CELEBRATE
CHRISTMAS?

EXPOSING THE
BABYLONIAN THREAD

DORA ADAMS

WestBow
PRESS®
A DIVISION OF THOMAS NELSON
& ZONDERVAN

WestBow Press books may be ordered through booksellers or by contacting:

WestBow Press
A Division of Thomas Nelson & Zondervan
1663 Liberty Drive
Bloomington, IN 47403
www.westbowpress.com
844-714-3454

Scripture taken from the King James Version of the Bible.

ISBN: 978-1-6642-3614-1 (sc)
ISBN: 978-1-6642-3615-8 (e)

Print information available on the last page.

WestBow Press rev. date: 09/17/2021

CONTENTS

ACKNOWLEDGEMENTS

I praise God from Whom all blessings flow…Looking unto Jesus who is the author and finisher of my faith.

I give God glory for providing me with insight and answers to my lifelong questions regarding the subject of this book.

I am forever grateful for my family, friends and my "special helper" who diligently worked to keep me encouraged throughout the years of my ministry. And all those who physically worked with me on this project.

FOREWORD

The celebration of Christmas disturbed me most of my life, yet I did not finally separate myself from it until I was in my late twenties. I had raised my first son, who was nine years older than my second to be realistic toward the holiday season, leaving out lies of Santa and the sleigh full of toys. We did however, exchange gifts with family members and prepared the holiday meal. The tree was not a regular fixture in our home, yet we would sometimes get one, just to set the mood for the holiday season. I was careful not to teach my son about Santa Clause, neither did I provide him with the alternate Christmas theory concerning the birth of Christ. For the most part, it was just a seasonal celebration for us. My younger children never participated in the winter festival at home. By the time they were born, I had become born-again and was seeking to serve the Lord with all my heart. When Jesus came into my life, He made me new. My whole perspective of existence changed, and I sought to make sense of it. This scripture became my reality; *"Therefore, if any man be in Christ, he is a new creature; old things are passed away; behold, all things are become new* (The Holy Bible, King James Version. Nashville, TN. 1976. Thomas Nelson. II Corinthians 5:17)." As I realized the profound change that was taking place in me, I found myself embracing the scripture for instruction as well as comfort. Meditating on the word gave me strength and I found myself growing up spiritually.

The Lord has given me this book, which is a ministry to the body of Christ, to compare truth from error and freedom from bondage.

With all my heart, I pray that this ministry will be a blessing and a cleansing to the church. The hour that we live in is extremely crucial. There are unprecedented events and activities taking place in all arenas of the world, setting the stage for the final conflict between the forces of darkness and the Kingdom of Heaven. We as believers on the earth must understand that we have a responsibility to our generation and to those who would come to Jesus because of our testimony in generations to come. Christians should be clean and holy before the Lord so that He can mightily demonstrate His power and authority through us on the earth. In these evil times in which we live, humanity will know that God is real. In the end, all nations will know that Jesus is Lord. His people will be ready for His return. We need to be ready to represent our King of Kings.

INTRODUCTION

My earliest memories take me back to warm scenes of wintery expectation in anticipation of the Christmas Holidays. As I recall, the festivities surrounding December 25th, began far in advance, and so did the excitement. From a very early age, I was trained to understand that we should celebrate Christmas. Being born into a family who identified themselves as "staunch" Episcopalians, I readily accepted the Christian teaching and training that they provided and believed within my heart that my elders were perfect. When it came to the things of God, the bible, and going to church, I knew that they could never be wrong. Surely, I felt confident in our "religion" and innocently participated in its practices. Every night in my grandparents' home everyone there would have to pray. We were instructed to gather into the dining room pull out the chairs and get on our knees. A book of prayers was passed around to those who could read, and my grandfather would assign passages to everyone. The prayers pointed to the sovereignty of God and the blessing of Jesus' sacrifice for humanity. Although my sister Pat and I did not understand the words that were spoken when we were young, we both felt a sense of peace when prayer time was over.

My grandfather was in his late 60's when I was a little girl. He had been a carpenter and bricklayer by trade, as well as an entrepreneur. His business partner was his younger brother. Together they worked successfully building and renovating homes. He took Pat and I to see vacant lots that he had purchased. We would run around and play while he walked the perimeter and extended his measuring device.

Sometime later, he would take us back there to see a newly built home. He was a very productive man and found pleasure in his craft. The basement (which we called the cellar) of his two-story home was where he worked. It was a large dark room filled with all kinds of tools. Granddaddy taught us the names of each gadget and we became familiar with its use. Often, we would go down the back staircase to talk to him as he worked. There was a strange odor in the air. Later we identified it as the smell of shaven wood. Sawdust covered the cellar floor, and our shoes always indicated where we had been. He made bookshelves, cabinets, and furniture for private customers, and was always "fixing things" around the house. Whether inside or outside of the home, my grandfather kept busy.

He planted flowers and shrubbery in his front yard, and mixed cement to pave the ground in the back of the house. I cannot remember a time that he was not working. When he reached retirement age, he and his brother dissolved their company. This gave my grandfather a lot of time on his hands. Pat, my constant companion, and I, enjoyed following him around as he occupied himself with various projects. He was the original male role model in our lives, even though his son was our father, we spent more time with my grandfather than any other family member. He loved us and we loved him.

My mother and father were not around during the daytime because they went to work. Our grandmother remained mostly indoors and supervised the housekeeping and food preparation. She too was in her late 60's and was not as active as we would have liked her to be. She basically sat around telling us stories from her past, and at times she would attempt to teach us how to read and write. Being of pre-school age, and full of energy we found it more fun to hang out with our grandfather. And if we stayed out of his way, that was fine with him. My father's sister whom we called Auntie was married and lived several miles from my grandparents' home. She had no children and was delighted when my mother and father allowed me to live with her. I am told that she became my guardian when I was nine months old. Both of my parents worked all day and had very little time to stay at home to watch the children. Pat lived with my grandparents. Auntie was a housewife, and because her parents were aging, we were at their home almost every day.

At three years old, I became conscious of the Christmas holiday season. There was a noticeable difference in the atmosphere. The adult's usual conversations took on a different character and the subjects were foreign to me. Auntie thought that it was very important to take me to Macy's on 34th Street in Manhattan, to see the window display. I remember much ceremony in getting ready to go. We had to have our hair just right and put on new outfits. The huge department store did not open early, so we had much of the day to get organized. As we prepared, we talked about Christmas, the snow, and Santa Clause. I was to see him at Macy's. Fear, mixed with anticipation, caused me to feel a bit anxious and somewhat stressed about meeting this unknown person. I was instructed to tell Santa what I wanted for Christmas when I saw him.

As the evening fell and the streetlights came on, we made our way to the train station. "Splish–splash" went the sound of my rubber boots as they touched the slush-filled sidewalk. Still not knowing what to expect, I followed Auntie as she guided me on and off, in and out, and up and down the way. Finally, we were there. Through the windows of Macy's, I was surprised to see highly decorated scenes with all sorts of toys. Some for girls and some for boys. Dolls of all sizes and colors, dressed up ever so lovely, were everywhere. Toy trains ran through a small town with houses, banks, stores and churches. There were lighted trees and frosty snowmen, dancing and waving to the onlookers. Artificial snow fell on the scenes as music box-like tunes filled the air. It was indeed a memorable sight, but that was just the beginning. I still had to see Santa.

He was quite elusive as I can recall. Auntie asked for directions to the North Pole. I could not understand what she meant, but with my hand in hers, I followed innocently. After a few short elevator and escalator rides, we finally found ourselves in a winter wonderland of reindeer madness. There were long lines of parents with children corralled behind ropes that I had only seen in the movie theater. The attendants, "Santa's Helpers," were working steadfastly to keep the line moving and console the crying children as they departed Santa's throne. A camera flash would occur periodically, and a new child would position himself on the strange character's lap. He wore a peculiar red suit, trimmed in white fur. His eyebrows and beard were thick and fuzzy. He appeared to be an old man, but Granddaddy was an old man, and so were some of the men in his church, but this Santa did not look like any of them. He was different. I noticed also that his face looked pale, and his cheeks were very red. He looked like a big toy or puppet, but I was encouraged to take him seriously. "Go ahead, it's your turn," one of the "helpers" would say as she pointed toward me. I held Auntie's hand as she escorted me to Santa's throne. I climbed on his lap and looked at his face and became dumbfounded. "Well, what's your name little girl?" My mouth would not open.

I could not say a word. I felt my fears turn into tears, so I turned away from him and looked out over the crowd of onlookers for my Auntie's face. When I made eye contact with her, she said, "Go on, tell him what you want. It's alright." I could not form a word. I was frozen. "Don't you want to get toys for Christmas?" she asked. I nodded yes. "Well, tell him what you want." The people in line began to get frustrated. The "helpers" came and took me down from his lap and put my hand into Auntie's hand. She was upset with me because I did not do what we had rehearsed. I told her that I could not do it because Santa Clause really scared me. I was glad to be finished with him anyway. She told me that I would not get anything for Christmas because I failed to tell Santa what I wanted. Secretly, I did not care. I was glad to be finished with him.

On the way home I noticed more and more creatures that looked like Santa Clause. There were fat ones with crisp, clean suits on, and there were thinner, even shorter Santa's. I thought about this and asked Auntie how come there were so many different Santa's. She told me that there was only one real Santa Clause who lived in the North Pole. The rest of them were his helpers. They all wanted to be like him, but there was only one real one. I wondered about her response. I then started to ask more and more questions. I could tell that Auntie was getting weary of me, but I was not going to be satisfied with trivial answers. I had been exposed to a strange new world and I wanted to know what it was about. I saw that she was frustrated, so, I made up my mind to ask Pat. She was two years older than me, and she knew everything. I thought Pat was the smartest person in the world.

When we got back home, the Christmas tree that stood in the middle of the living room floor, near the window caught my attention. There were plenty of them in Macy's and along the streets in front of houses. The lights went on when the plug went into the socket on the wall. It was pretty to look at but dangerous because the light bulbs got very hot. I was told never touch the lights because I could get burned. I stood far away from the Christmas tree. My mind searched for meaning to all this Christmas stuff. There were wrapped presents under the tree. We could not open them until Christmas. Auntie said that one of them was for me because it had my name on it, and I wondered what was in it. Auntie would pick up the packages and shake them and listen to the sound they made. She was so excited. We had to get ready for bed because Santa Clause was coming to our house. She told me that he was going to come down the chimney and put toys under the tree. I did not expect to get anything from Santa. I never told him what I wanted. "What will he bring me?" I thought, and "Where is the chimney?"

The next morning, I awoke early to seek out more information on Santa Clause. "Did he really come last night?" As I made my way down the stairs, I saw Auntie fussing over the presents. She gave me the box that she showed me the night before, the one with my name on it. "Open It," she said. I did just that. It was a pretty, new dress. She told me to put it on and get ready to go to my grandparents' home. "Did Santa come last night?" I asked. "Yep," she replied. "He took all of the toys to Grandaddy's house. He knew that we would be going over there today."

I was glad to be going to Grandaddy's because Pat was there. She would help me understand. By early afternoon we arrived, and I can recall the excitement building up as we rang the doorbell at the foot of the stairs. Pat was the first to respond, by pressing the buzzer at the top of the staircase, which opened the door. As we climbed the stairs, I could smell freshly baked bread and sweet potato pie. I also detected a Christmas tree because of the fragrance of pine in the air. The scene in the dining room of my grand-parent's home had changed since I had been there last. The table in the center of the room was set to perfection with the best china and silverware that my grandmother had. Everyone was talking and appearing to have fun, but I sensed that something was wrong. I recall feeling a sadness in the air.

Pat was happy. She was so excited about seeing me and what Santa had brought her. I asked her if he came, and she said yes. I then wanted to know where the chimney was. She took me upstairs to the attic, into a small corridor that led to the back of the house. She opened a short door with a glass knob. Inside, there was a brick wall. "See, that's the chimney," she said. "How did Santa come through there?" I asked. "I don't know, it's some kind of magic," Pat replied. She tried to get my mind away from thinking about the details as we hurriedly descended the stairs and appeared back into the dining room.

The Christmas tree was considerably larger than the tree we had in our house. It filled the front room. It was taller than the doorway and its top reached the ceiling. The branches were decorated with shiny balls, lights, and tinsel. There was a white webbing that resembled the beard of Santa Clause spread all over the tree. Pat told me that it was called "Angel hair." "Don't touch it," she said. "it will make you itch all day." I did not want to itch. I had the chicken pox before and did not want to feel like that again.

As the guests arrived, Pat and I raced to the top of the stairs to ring the buzzer to let them in. The first thing they did when they settled in was admire the tree and compliment my grandmother on her cozy home. She always took time to make things nice and comfortable for her friends and family. I noticed that my grandfather was somewhat unhappy. He seemed out of place in the middle of the festivities. The adults and children were all chatting, laughing, drinking and eating. Soon, Grandaddy gathered everyone in the house, young and old, into the living room and cut the lights down low. I thought that he was going to lead us into prayer, but he did not. He sat on the piano bench and began to play the old piano that stood in the sun parlor. He requested that we all sing Christmas songs. Auntie suggested that we sing "Rudolph the Red Nose Reindeer," and "Santa Clause is Coming to Town," but my grandfather said, "No, it's Christmas and we are going to sing Christmas songs. The religious ones." We sang, "O Holy Night," "Silent Night," and "Hark the Herald Angels Sing." This seemed to satisfy my grandfather, who wanted to keep the focus of Christmas on Jesus Christ and his birth. Auntie wanted to lighten the mood of the celebration, by adding a few of her suggestions, but Grandaddy said, "No. "Christmas is about Jesus, not that other foolishness." After that we prayed and ate the delicious meal that my grandmother had prepared. At the time I could not make the connection between Jesus and Santa Claus, but I left it alone and decided to play with Pat.

IS CHRISTMAS FOR CHRISTIANS

Time seemed to move quickly during my formative years. Just prior to the time that I was to enter kindergarten, my parents decided to take me back to live with them. This decision devastated Auntie and caused me to become very depressed. She was like a mother to me, and I was used to her nurturing manner. My mother tried her best to boost my morale, and my father was overjoyed to have me back in their home. He wanted his family to be together and wanted to reclaim Pat also but succumbed to his aging parents' wishes to let her stay with them. As the seasons came and went, I had many questions about life that needed to be answered. Being a close-knit family, we continued to share church attendance, family dinners, outings, and the celebration of holidays.

The scenes that I described in the preceding pages of this book continued to take place each Christmas. When new children were born into the family, they too were introduced to Santa Claus during the Christmas season. I recall being confused about Santa Clause and wondered what exactly he had to do with Jesus. The adults tried to explain away my concerns by saying that Jesus was truly born on Christmas day and because the three kings came and gave Jesus presents, we should give presents to one another. But what about Santa? No one could give me a sufficient answer, until one day, when I was about six, my sister Pat told me that she found out that Santa Claus was not real. He was just a made-up story to trick the kids. "Why would they want to trick the kids?" I thought. We have been betrayed. I became determined that I would never lie to my kids or try to deceive them. I planned on telling them the truth. This was the first instance of distrust that I felt towards my elders. If they lied to me about Santa, what else are they lying about? In the years following, I began to despise the fantasy of "Christmas." I leaned more toward my grandfather's religious perspective and took Christmas more seriously considering the birth of Jesus. I enjoyed the nativity plays, the songs, and the candlelight services in church on Christmas Eve. I tried to keep in mind the reason for the season.

When I was in the sixth grade, the teachers decided to do an onstage production of "A Christmas Carol," by Charles Dickens. I was a member of the chorus and we sang different kinds of Christmas songs. "Silver Bells," "Have Yourself a Merry Little Christmas," "It's Beginning to Look a Lot Like Christmas" and "Deck the Halls." The lyrics to these tunes were quite different than, "Silent Night," "It Came upon a Midnight Clear" and "O Holy Night," which pointed to the birth of Christ. These songs were light, happy and universal. I was uncomfortable about the mixture of themes during the winter holiday season. Still wanting to adhere to the nativity story, I rejected all other explanations of Christmas.

I began to see the Christmas season as a tool for commercial gain as well. The adults talked about how much money they had spent on gifts for those who were on their lists. Negativity was expressed when some found out that they did not get a gift in return from someone they gave a gift to. Underlying bad attitudes ran parallel with the feigned joy of the season. I also noticed an irritation that followed the Christmas spirit, as many overextended themselves financially in preparation for the holidays. It was a time when rationality and responsibility seemed to be suspended. Many spent their rent money and neglected to pay their bills in order to satisfy the requests of their children and other loved ones.

There was a lot of cooking, eating and drinking during the week between Christmas Eve and New Year's Day. With the gathering of friends and family, many a memory was created during this time of the year. There were also those who became depressed because they had no one to share this special time with. There were others that I knew who found it unbearable to make it through the season because of heartfelt pain. Some having no family to enjoy the holiday with. For many older people, Christmas was a very sad time because it reminded them of their past. Memories of cherished times of celebrating the holidays with family and friends were all that remained. Thoughts of deceased loved ones made it difficult for them to get through Christmas. Others who were less fortunate felt inadequate because they did not have money to buy gifts or toys for their children. This contributed to their feeling of despair. I learned as time went on that the Christmas holiday season produced increased suicides. Death tolls rose as well because of increased criminal activity and alcohol and other drug consumption. Indeed, I found that the Christmas season did not render joy and happiness to everyone.

In contrast to the celebrations of the season many people grieved. My closest friend was very sad when December arrived. She told me that she hated the holidays because so many of her relatives had passed away during that month. Memories of funerals and mourning would not release her to enjoy the celebrations. Her home felt gloomy, and the mood was depressing. Her entire family found the Christmas season to be extremely uncomfortable. Because of this, in the back of my mind, I found myself even more disturbed with the winter holiday as well. The only good thing about it were the ten days off from school and the delicious culinary delights that were prepared for the celebration. By the age of fifteen, I decided not to go along with the hype of the holiday. I stopped trying to act cheerful and I stopped being concerned about gift giving. When questioned about my position, I openly shared my thoughts about the matter. Of course, many who were close to me disagreed strongly. I found that so many were thoroughly convinced that Christmas was Jesus' birthday, and tried to make me understand the importance of honoring Him through participation in the celebration.

The older generation of my family passed away and my parents were not as strict as theirs. Going to church was not mandatory anymore. As a family we all fell away from religious training. When the Christmas season came, it gave way to a time of feasting, drinking and hanging out with friends and family. Economically, it was not always feasible to exchange gifts with every individual and for the most part, the children were supplied with new toys. I discerned a sense of darkness during the winter celebration. The atmosphere seemed dreary, and it was almost always cloudy, rainy or snowy. In New York, preparations were made for bad weather and activities were planned for indoors. Playing games, dancing, or just hanging out was the norm.

The time arrived in my life that I was expecting a child. I was twenty-one and recall having a heart-to-heart talk with my mother. I was facing the responsibility for the life of another human being and I knew that it was very important to take my role as a parent seriously. I recall discussing with her my concerns about motherhood. The subject of being truthful with my child came up. "I don't want to lie to my kid." I told my mother. "What do you mean?" "Why would anyone want to lie to their own child?" she inquired. "You know how parents lie to their children about Christmas, Santa Clause, the Easter Bunny and things like that?" I replied. She looked at me and saw that I was serious, almost in tears. "Well, when you have your child, you will feel different. Every parent wants the best for their children and so will you. Telling him about Santa Clause is not really a lie, it's just a story, like fable or fiction." "But fiction is a lie." I thought in my mind. "Children need to know the truth. This way, they will be able to grow up smart, not relying on foolishness," I said. My mother held her peace. She somehow ended with, "We'll see what you do with your own baby." When my son was born, I took my position as a parent very seriously. I knew that I would be accountable for his life. I was very adamant about not participating in the holiday festivities.

While in college, I moved near my Auntie. She had been my guardian when I was very young, and I remained close to her over the years. Her influence overshadowed my choice and I found myself decorating, cooking and shopping for Christmas. Because she enjoyed the fanfare so much, I gave it a try. I enjoyed the fellowship that I had with her shopping, cooking and preparing for guests. My son was endowed with gifts from my Auntie and Uncle and looked forward to getting presents for Christmas. I was told that it was cruel to deprive him of his fun, by not giving him lots of toys. So, I went along with the program and provided him with as much as my budget could afford as well. After a few years I learned to phase out the celebration once again. I was not comfortable and felt continually disturbed by participating.

In my late twenties I was introduced to the gospel of Jesus Christ, which opened a whole new experience for me. I began reading the bible and inquiring about the things of God. The church I attended was a major denomination which focused on teaching. It was through this experience that I began to get a new perspective on life and God. I learned that there exist good and evil forces operating in the lives of humans on earth. Both powers, attempted to get complete control over all people. Those who were victorious in this cosmic struggle were the ones who found their way to God through Jesus Christ. These simple truths expanded my understanding about life and especially myself. Immediately, I was propelled to investigate the origin of Christmas and all that surrounded the birth of Jesus Christ, a subject that disturbed me for years. My desire was to know the truth. I prayed for wisdom, knowledge and understanding. The Lord has answered my prayer.

THE TRUTH WILL MAKE YOU FREE

A s a new Christian, determined to know God's will for my life, I became very familiar with the bible. Soon, I realized that I was not alone in my search, the Lord Himself was working with me, providing me with the answers that I sought. As I learned how God dealt with mankind from the beginning in the Garden of Eden, I understood that He still operates the same way. God is God. The Almighty. The maker and creator of all things that exists. He is without repentance. *God is not man, that he should lie; neither the son of man, that He should repent: hath He said, and shall He not do it? Or hath he spoken, and shall He not make it good* (Numbers 23:19)? *For I am the Lord, I change not: therefore, ye sons of Jacob are not consumed* (Malachi 3:6). *Every good and perfect gift is from above, and cometh down from the father of lights, with whom is no variableness, neither shadow of turning* (James 1:17).

Through much study, observation and experience, I began to know within myself that the bible was an historical reality and that it was God's communication to mankind. I decided to dedicate myself to extensive study and research to make sense of the battle between good and evil. I found that the way in which God deals with the reality of sin and iniquity (lawlessness) remains the same. God is light and life. He pours out or dispenses His life onto and into believers. Throughout the ages of earth's history, God has poured out of His spirit, infilling and empowering man with abilities above that which is available from the natural realm. My thoughts continually turned inward to examine my personal motives and intentions. The light of the truth illuminated my world, I knew for sure that God was as real as any other living being, and that I was called to make known the things that He revealed to me.

As I learned about God's plan of salvation through Jesus Christ, I came to grips with my responsibility to share the good news. To do this, effectively, I had to understand the scripture, and allow the Holy Spirit to teach me the details of God's way of righteousness. I was called into ministry in my mid-thirties, over thirty years ago.

LED BY THE SPIRIT INTO ALL TRUTH

Thy word have I hid in my heart that I might not sin against thee (Psalm 119:11). As believers, we must first put the word of God in our hearts and teach our children to do so as well. This way, we will not do things just because everyone else is doing them. We will understand what pleases God and what displeases Him. There are many things that appear to be innocent, but they are wicked in the sight of God. That is why humans need the Holy Spirit's leading. *Howbeit when He, the Spirit of truth is come, He will guide you into all truth* (John 16:13). Naturally, humans are not prepared to hear the voice of God, nor do they grasp the depth of His word. Mankind stems from the seed of Adam, and because of the sinful nature of Adam, all humans are born intrinsically sinners having a fallen nature. The interpretation of life, prior to salvation is derived from the senses as we touch the world. When God intervenes in our hearts and opens the way of communication we respond to a higher level of existence. This is when the Spirit of Truth comes. If we follow His leading, we will know the truth and find that other voices and concepts concerning man's existence and destiny are false.

Get wisdom, get understanding; forget it not; neither decline from the words of my mouth (Proverbs 4:5). Once God has our attention, and we choose to listen, He then tells us to get wisdom. From God's perspective:

The fear of the Lord is the beginning of wisdom (Proverbs 9:10). We are responsible for our gaining wisdom. The fear of the Lord based on His truth and His reality will make a person wise. Those who do not fear the Lord, nor desire to know and adhere to his Truth makes them foolish. *Wisdom is the principal thing, therefore, get wisdom* (Proverbs 4:7). The principal thing is the first thing of importance. In order of rank in obtaining the truth of God's word, having a proper fear of the Lord is the first thing. *And with all thy getting, get understanding* (Proverbs 4:7). The bible defines itself...*The knowledge of the Holy is understanding* (Proverbs 9:10). Getting to know God, who is Holy, will bring believers into a perfect understanding of His purpose and plan for His people, as well as for the world.

The bible teaches that we are bought with a price, the atoning blood of Jesus Christ, and that God chose us to serve Him. We did not come up with that idea on our own. Believers are called into the Kingdom and household of God. We are adopted as sons and are joint heirs with Christ. The bible gives us instruction to be transformed by the renewing of our minds. As stated earlier, the natural man is born in sin and is subject to the knowledge of his environment as interpreted by the flesh, under the influence of Satan. The sacrifice that Jesus made on the cross at Calvary, paid the price for the sin of the whole world. Each individual person is given the opportunity to come out of Satan's kingdom of bondage to the flesh and enter God's kingdom of life and liberty by His Spirit.

No longer are those who have accepted God's plan of salvation through Jesus Christ to partake in the fruitless works of darkness. We are taught that the world is in darkness and we have been translated out of the world. The rules of the world are set by Satan. The laws governing the Kingdom of Heaven are set by God. Believers must live by the laws and commandments of God because in them there is life and liberty while the powers of darkness only offer sin and death.

The Apostle Paul states *"And you hath he quickened, who were dead in trespasses and sins; Wherein in times past ye walked according to the course of this world, according to the prince of the power of the air, the spirit that now works in the children of disobedience: Among whom also we all had our conversation in times past in the lusts of our flesh and of the mind; and were by nature the children of wrath, even as others* (Ephesians 2:1-3)." We all have been born into this sinful world, and by nature as sinners, we need to be cleansed and reconciled to God. This is the reason He sent Jesus. Paul continues, *"But God, who is rich in mercy, for His great love wherewith he loved us, even when we were dead in sins, hath quickened us together with Christ, (by grace ye are saved) and hath raised us up together and made us sit together in heavenly places in Christ Jesus* (Ephesians 2:4-6)."

The word of God, the bible, brings light to our "new creature" status. Even though we look the same, we have been changed when we accept Jesus into our lives. It is our responsibility to manifest the change by living a life for God, according to His truth and His standards. We are to allow the word of God and the Holy Spirit to teach us how to be conformed to heavenly kingdom living and thinking. We cannot rely on what we have extracted out of the world, because the world is in darkness. We must get all understanding from God and see things from His perspective. The new believer must learn to yield. This means letting the Lord have His way in our lives without resistance.

As we place ourselves in the hands of our Heavenly Father, He can shape us and make us into His masterpiece. This process begins with a willing heart. There exist so much confusion among believers because there is no unity of purpose among them. This is not God's will. His desire is for believers in Christ to grow up and be fully matured. We, as the body, must recognize that Jesus Christ is the head. The church makes up the individual members of the body and function as a unit. The body cannot function if the unit is not in unity. Therefore, the Holy Spirit must work to bring about unity in the body of Christ. Bringing together all believers on one accord and in agreement with the word of God is the ministry of the Holy Spirit.

Howbeit when He, the spirit of truth is come, He will guide you into all truth (John 16:13). The Holy Spirit is our guide through the bible. He also places each member into the body of Christ. *For by one Spirit, are we all baptized into one body…* (I Corinthians 12:13). God has also provided the church, with able ministers to help the body get nourished and grow. *And he gave some, apostles; and some, prophets; and some, evangelist; and some, pastors; and teachers; for the perfecting of the saints, for the work of the ministry, for the edifying of the body of Christ: Till we all come in the unity of the faith, and the knowledge of the Son of God, unto a perfect man, unto the measure of the stature of the fullness of Christ* (Ephesians 4:11-13).

Renewing our minds, yielding our lives and allowing the Holy Spirit to work to build us up in Christ is the responsibility of the church. God has made the provision for our transformation. We must utilize all that we have been given to become the manifestation of the children of God. *That we henceforth be no more children, tossed to and fro and carried about with every wind of doctrine by the sleight of men, and cunning craftiness, whereby they lie in wait to deceive* (Ephesians 4:14). Babies and young children are incapable of moving on their own. They cannot reach a desired destination without assistance. Young ones need the help of others to get around. Because they have little weight, they can be unstable and fall. Children and unlearned ones can be deceived by anyone. The influence of deceitful men empowered by the darkness of this world can cause many to be entrapped on the broad way that leads to death. *Enter ye in at the strait gate: for wide is the gate, and broad is the way, that leadeth to destruction, and many there be which go in thereat:* (Matthew 7:13). It is the responsibility of every believer to come to grips with their life in Christ Jesus and become all that God has ordained them to be.

When I accepted Jesus as my personal Savior and asked Him to come into my life and be the head of my life, He did. I did not know what to expect, as I followed the instructions given to me by the Lord, in faith. I was led into intensive study of the scripture and spent several years in the books of Daniel and Revelation. Through these two books, the Lord was able to minister to me His purpose and plans for His people. Every question that I could think of was answered through scripture. All the answers are in the bible. As my understanding increased, my love toward God increased. I saw how much He loved the seed of Adam, the fallen man, to the extent that He provided a way of restoration. I learned how much He hated sin and how He made a way through Jesus' life, death and resurrection, for humans to experience a new birth, a sinless nature washed and cleansed in the blood of the Lamb. I appreciated all that God had done for me and I will continue to give Him praise for giving me Jesus.

The bible tells us that if you draw near to God, He will draw near to you. This is a true statement. When God is near to you, He imparts

His life into you. You become more and more like Him. I noticed my life changing because I knew what the word of God said, and I believed it. I began to be conscious of abomination and wickedness in the world. As I studied and continued to seek the Lord for answers and purpose, He showed me His desire for His people.

DECEPTION

The fall of man brought separation from God and the Garden of Eden. From the moment that judgement was placed on Adam, Eve and the Serpent; the whole earth plunged into darkness. Adam gave his dominion over the earth to Satan. In turn, the deceiver became the god of this world. Satan's term of office was not without limitation. God told him that He would place enmity between him and the woman, as well as their seed. This meant that there was to be born of a woman a human that would contend for the authority over the earth once again. The contest was on since then. We see throughout scripture, Satan's effortless struggle to maintain his authority over all of God's creation.

The seed of the woman was Jesus, who existed before the foundation of the world. He was pointed to, prophetically, in the law and the prophets of the Old Testament as … *the shadow of things to come...* (Hebrews 10:1). He entered the earth in the New Testament and completed the dethroning of Satan by fulfilling the prophetic death on the cross, and the shedding of His blood for the atonement of the sin of the whole world. Jesus *spoiled principalities and powers and made a show of them openly* (Colossians 2:15). He overthrew the enemy of mankind and demonstrated Satan's defeat by stripping him of his power and authority. Jesus also performed a death-defying victory over all that Satan had. He defeated death, hell, and the grave. He broke the power of darkness by giving light to the world. He gave strength to the weak, health to the infirm, sight to the blind and freedom to the captive. The prophet

Isaiah spoke of the mission of Jesus in the Old Testament, and Luke records Jesus' reiteration of His purpose in the New Testament. *The Spirit of the Lord is upon me because he hath anointed me to preach the gospel to the poor; he hath sent me to heal the brokenhearted, to preach deliverance to the captives, and recovering of sight to the blind, to set at liberty them that are bruised...* (Luke 4:18).

Most importantly, Jesus paved the way for humans to return to God the Father in a pure, loving and living relationship. The heavens were now opened, and the voice of man could be heard in the kingdom. Not only his voice, but his life could be found in heavenly places in Christ Jesus, totally restored with power, ability, righteousness and holiness.

Satan knew the holy nature of God. He knew also that no unclean thing could enter in the Kingdom of Heaven. In his defeated state, he continued to exercise rule over humans, utilizing man's ignorance to the ways of God. Humans know how to live for the devil because they are naturally born in sin, however, when salvation comes to us through our acceptance of Jesus Christ, we must learn the ways of God and yield ourselves to walk in them. Satan's campaign was to keep humans in darkness and uncleanness by counterfeiting Jesus, the scripture and the gospel message. He took advantage of man and caused many to follow him blindly, thinking they were serving God. The counterfeit appears real outwardly, on the surface, but when you look past the veneer, you can see more clearly. Satan has kept millions of God's people in darkness because he was able to trick them to continue in sin. The very things God hates are the things that Satan uses to entice humans. He has kept up a system of religious deception that has destroyed the lives of many would-be believers and God allows it to happen. Why? Because He wants man to seek Him, love Him, and serve Him by choice, not by obligation. If there was no option, we would have no choice, but now we can choose to follow God or Satan. How will we know the difference? We will have to know God's voice and His word.

The celebration of Christmas is just one area that Satan has successfully tricked believers into separating themselves from God. There are many others. *The Babylonian Thread that Runs Through* is a concept that I have researched and written to expose many deceptions that Satan has devised to keep believers in Christ alienated from Gods kingdom. It is the believer's responsibility to discern truth from error and be received by our Father. *Be ye not unequally yoked together with unbelievers: for what fellowship hath righteousness with unrighteousness? and what communion hath light with darkness? And what concord hath Christ with Belial? or what part hath he that believeth with an infidel? And what agreement hath the temple of God with idols? for ye are the temple of the living God; as God hath said, I will dwell in them, and walk in them; and I will be their God, and they shall be my people* (II Corinthians 14-16). A clear distinction must be made, will believers serve God, or will they continue to serve the devil? The individual must make the choice. The scripture reads, *wherefore come out from among them, and be ye separate, saith the Lord, and touch not the unclean thing; and I will receive you, and will be a Father unto you, and ye shall be my sons and daughters, saith the Lord Almighty* (II Corinthians 6:17,18).

THE AUTHORITY OF THE WORD

Jesus told His disciples what it would take to be made free from all deception. *If ye continue in my word, then ye are my disciples, indeed; And ye shall know the truth, and the truth shall make you free* (John 8:31). Born again believers should have one goal in their daily existence and that is to know the truth. Everything in life, whether it be abstract or concrete, must be examined considering God's word. The mind of God is expressed in the scriptures and it is vital that all believers familiarize themselves with the bible. It is through this process of learning that one can be firmly rooted in the way of righteousness. King David knew this. He was a man after the heart of God. He wrote, *Thy word have I hid in my heart, that I might not sin against thee* (Psalm 119:11). The humble king had found the key to pleasing God.

Remember, believers are commanded to *"get knowledge... get wisdom..., and with all of our getting, get understanding* (Proverbs 4:7). Christians must set our hearts on obtaining all that God wants us to have. Believers must be open and receptive to the truths found in scripture because, understanding is knowledge of the holy nature of God. Many professed Christians fail to comprehend this aspect when they come to God for Salvation. He gives it to them freely; not only by way of cleansing them from sin, but also by giving them a new life. They ask Jesus to come into their hearts and to be head of their lives, and they stop at that. They have no clue as to the depths of truth that the Lord desires to impart to them. This must be changed. All those who name the name Jesus Christ as their Lord, Savior and head, must take seriously the nature of their new life. *Therefore, if any man be in Christ, he is a new creature: old things are passed away; behold all things are become new* (II Corinthians 5:17). Newborn believers are babies, needing to be nurtured, fed and raised in a way of holiness and true righteousness in order to experience life in the kingdom of Heaven.

Too much responsibility has been left in the hands of pastors and church leaders. For the most part, Christians have become dependent on the teaching and instructions of other humans, many of whom are not matured, equipped, nor led by the Spirit of God. New birth is delicate. When a new baby is born to parents that love him, he will be nurtured, trained and raised to assimilate into the family. That child will express the culture, habits and attitudes of the parents, until he develops and is able to go on his own. The father and/or mother, have the responsibility of rearing the child and preparing that child to face life. It is the same for the new birth into the Kingdom of God. New believers should put their trust in the Lord only. The body of Christ has been stunted in growth because of this. The Holy Spirit, and His representatives, the five-fold-ministry, should be the only teacher to the church. Jesus said, *"Howbeit when He, The Spirit of Truth is come, He will guide you into all truth: for He shall not speak of Himself; but whatsoever He shall hear, that shall He speak... and He will show you things to come* (John 16:13)."* It is important that every believer comprehend the necessity of turning their life over to the Lord Jesus Christ knowing that, through Him, God has made all provisions for growth and development through the word and by the leading of His Spirit. Following the Spirit of Truth will ensure progress toward living a life that will glorify God on earth, as well as making preparation to live in the Kingdom of Heaven with Jesus. The Apostle Peter called believers to understand their identity in Christ, *"But ye are a chosen generation, a royal priesthood, a holy nation, a peculiar people; that ye should shew forth the praises of Him who has called you out of darkness into His marvelous light* (I Peter 2:9)."*

The enemy, Satan does not want believers to realize their status as "new creatures." He has set up a system of deception to slow down their growth, as well as destroy their lives. He has mastered a clever plan, thousands of years ago and it has been successful in causing the downfall of many people who have put their hope and trust in the true and living God. This evil system is called, "religion." For a human to escape the grip and penalty of sin, he must be saved. This process begins with believing that God sent His only begotten Son, Jesus, into the world to be the propitiation for the sin of mankind. His death on the cross and the shedding of his blood, satisfied the penalty for sin and made the atonement for the whole world. *For God so loved the world, that He gave His only begotten Son, that whosoever believeth in Him, should not perish, but have everlasting life* (John 3:16). Religion is contrary to faith, or simply believing and accepting what God has done through Jesus. Religion involves a systematic structured culture, in which its adherents have faith in. The Bible tells us to have faith in God, but religion causes one to have faith in an organization, culture, tradition or human. When people attempt to have control over the things of God, they will not be successful. God must be in control. In His omnipotence He extends grace to all who will believe.

I have inquired of the Lord in prayer and scripture, the answer to the challenges that face new believers, as well as those who have been saved a long time. Why is there so much confusion among Christians? Why are there so many denominations? Why don't all Christians speak the same thing? These questions troubled me for years and as I grew closer to the Lord in my personal relationship, they troubled me even more.

The answers came by revelation. When the Lord began to make plain to me the source of the confusion, I was shocked. He led me into the study of ancient Babylon and then revealed to me that Babylon is still in operation. It is still a governing force in the world and that is why there is mention of it in the last book of the bible, Revelation. It took many years to get the full picture, but the Holy Spirit, the *Spirit of Truth*, continued to guide me. The culmination of my studies and a series of revelations brought me to the bottom line. The religious system of Babylon, originated by Satan himself, has evolved into the highly sophisticated and complicated organized institution designed to hinder the growth of God's people and hinder their entrance into the Kingdom.

Jesus' shed blood cleanses us from all unrighteousness. Those who are found in the household of faith by the redeeming blood of the Lamb have access to the Father. Jesus announced, *"I am the way, the truth and the life; no man cometh unto the Father but by me* (John 14:6)." Therefore, ultimate truth is found in Jesus Christ. *In the beginning was the Word, and the Word was with God, and the Word was God. The same was in the beginning with God. All things were made by Him and without Him was not anything made that was made. In Him was life; and the life was the light of men* (John 1:1-4). Jesus is the Word, the same from before the foundation of the world. It is by the Word and through the Word that we have truth. Jesus prayed for our consecration. *Sanctify them through thy truth; thy Word is truth* (John 17:17).

CONCERNING THE BIRTH OF JESUS

Now the birth of Jesus was on this wise: When His mother, Mary, was espoused to Joseph, before they came together, she was found with child of the Holy Ghost. Then Joseph, her husband, being a just man and not willing to make her a public example, was minded to put her away privily. However, while he thought on these things, behold, the angel of the Lord appeared unto him in a dream, saying, "Joseph, thou son of David, fear not to take unto thee Mary thy wife: for that which is conceived in her is of the Holy Ghost. And she shalt bring forth a son, and thou shalt call his name Jesus; for he shall save his people from their sins." Now, all this was done that it might be fulfilled which was spoken of the Lord by the prophet saying, "Behold a virgin shall be with child, and shall bring forth a son, and they shall call his name Emanuel, which being interpreted is God is with us (Matthew 1:18-23)."

There is not a word in the bible about the precise day of the birth of Jesus, or the time of the year that He was born. However, the statements recorded in the bible clearly indicate that it could not have been on December 25th. When the announcement of the angel came to the shepherds at Bethlehem, they were feeding their flocks, at night, in the open fields. *And there were in the same country shepherds abiding in the field, keeping watch over their flock by night. And, lo, the angel of the Lord came upon them, and the glory of the Lord shone around them; and they were sore afraid. And the angel said unto them, "Fear not; for, behold, I bring you tidings of great joy, which shall be to all people. For unto you is born this day in the city of David, a Savior, which is Christ the Lord"* (Luke 2:8-11).

The word "abide" means to live, reside, or continue to be in a place for a noticeable time. The biblical account concerning the birth of Christ illustrates that the time that He was born was during the season that the shepherds lived in the fields as they kept watch over their sheep. The climate in Palestine is not as severe in the winter as it is in some parts of the United States, however there is a noticeable drop in temperatures. The weather in December gets even colder at night and is often rainy, cloudy and windy. The shepherds would bring in their flocks from the fields no later than October in preparation for the cold of winter. Another clue that can be uncovered in proving that Jesus was not born on the 25th of December is found in Luke's account of the mandatory taxation ordered by Augustus Caesar. At the time that Jesus was born, His parents, Mary and Joseph were not at their home in Galilee. They were responding to the announcement that required everyone to return to their place of origin to be taxed. They journeyed from their current place of residence to the city of Bethlehem where Joseph was born, and Mary was about to deliver her child.

And it came to pass that in those days, that there went out a decree from Caesar Augustus, that the world should be taxed (And this taxing was first made when Cyrenius was governor of Syria). And all went to be taxed, everyone into his own city. And Joseph also went up from Galilee, out of the city of Nazareth, unto Judea, unto the city of David, which is called Bethlehem; (because he was one of the house and lineage of David) to be taxed with Mary, his espoused wife, being great with child. And so, it was that while they were there, the days were accomplished that she should be delivered. And she brought forth her firstborn son, and wrapped him in swaddling clothes, and laid him in a manger because there was no room for them at the inn (Luke 2:1-7).

The subject of the decree to "tax all the world" is especially important to examine in the light of the time of Jesus' birth. The declaration went out that all should be taxed and that every person must go to the city of their birth to pay their taxes. This required traveling for the entire population. It is not likely that the governor would intentionally impose the hardship of the journey on families, especially women and children. Everyone was expected to comply with the decree, no matter how far they had to travel. This could not have taken place in the winter.

It is hardly likely that the ruler of Rome would order a decree for all to be taxed in the winter. As the order went out, it was a requirement for all people to respond. This would have called for major travel plans for all citizens. It would have been extremely difficult for some to make the journey due to the weather restrictions. And it would have been especially difficult for women and children. Therefore, we can figure that such a decree was not given during the winter month of December. Jesus discussed with His disciples the hardship of traveling in winter when He spoke to them about the events that will take place at the end of the age. He told them to *"...Pray that your flight not be in winter...* (Matthew 24:20)." Considering the shepherds in the fields, and the massive travel required for the taxation, we can understand that these events did not happen in late December.

Joseph Mede, who studied the aspects of the subject of Jesus' birth on the December 25th holiday during the 1600's, points out among other arguments: "At the birth of Christ, every man, woman, and child was to be taxed at the city whereto they belonged, within some had long journeys but the middle of the winter was not fitting for such business, especially for women with their child or children to travel in." Hislop, Alexander, The Two Babylons, Neptune, NJ. 1959, Loizeaux Brothers, Inc. 92

God, in His sovereignty, knows the end from the beginning. That is why He provided in His word the inalterable account of the events surrounding the birth of Jesus. There was no room at the inn, indicates that the time of Joseph's trip to Bethlehem of Judea from his residence in Nazareth, was during peak travel season. These clues indicate that Jesus was not born during the winter month of December. We must acknowledge also that the scriptures do not tell us when it was that Jesus' birth occurred. There is no mention in scripture about the date of Jesus' birth, neither is there any suggestion or command that believers celebrate His birthday.

"No one knows the exact day that Jesus was born, but, in all probability, he was born sometime during the first part of October... Because His earthly ministry lasted 3 1/2 years and he was crucified on the fourteenth day of the month of Nisan, which corresponds to our April (John 19:31, Leviticus 23:5). If we go back 3 ½ years, to the time Jesus was 30 years old – when He began His public ministry, we come to the month of October. This was probably the month

when our blessed Lord was born into the world. "However, let us remember that it's not the date of Jesus' birth that's important. The important thing is that He was born and that He died for our sins. We are not worshipping a helpless infant lying in a manger. We are worshipping a risen and exalted Christ who has all power in Heaven and earth." Halff, Charles, The Truth About Christmas, Christian Jew Foundation, p.3. It must be admitted that no one knows the date of Jesus' birthday. Scripture provides us with clues that prevent our agreement that it was during the winter season on December 25th.

In the Old Testament, there were several feasts that the Hebrews were commanded to observe through the law given to Moses. All those observances were symbolic pointing to the coming savior, Jesus the Christ, and prophesied of His life. When He was born, He fulfilled that which was spoken of in types and shadows. His birth and life were not a continuation of the Old testament law, but rather the manifestation of all that it pointed to. Nowhere in scripture can be found the doctrine of celebrating birthdays. Jesus did not speak of His own birth, neither did He encourage people to focus on His personal life. He did not make a big deal about who He was, rather, ...*Who, being in the form of God, thought it not robbery to be equal with God; But made Himself of no reputation, and took upon Him the form of a servant, and was made in the likeness of men: And being found in fashion as a man, He humbled Himself, and became obedient unto death, even the death of the cross* (Philippians 2:6-8). Jesus made no reputation of Himself. He was obedient to the will of the Father throughout His life, all the way to His death on the cross. We see no indication in scripture that Jesus celebrated His birth, neither is there any indication that He disobeyed the will of God. Therefore, if Christmas were a biblical festival, it would have been written in the scripture and Jesus would have taught and practiced it.

We can conclude, therefore, that the celebration of Christmas is not a holiday for believers in Christ, neither are its practices of biblical origin. The testimony of the birth of Christ, given in scripture, by the law, through types and shadows, by the prophets, through prophetic unction, and by the accounts of the New Testament writers, prove that the celebration of the day called Christmas has nothing to do with Jesus of the Bible. Given the facts of scripture and the examination of the conditions surrounding the birth of Christ, the winter festival called

Christmas, recognized all over the world, must have its roots in sources outside of God. It is our duty to present evidence as to the origin of Christmas and supply the reader with sufficient reasons to choose not to participate.

THE ORIGIN OF THE WINTER FESTIVAL

Christmas, as we know it, was originally a pagan celebration. Pagans are the people who were not in covenant with God, they were also referred to as nations or heathens. Most of the pagan religions were polytheistic, believing in more than one god. Most of the gods of the heathen were ascribed to some aspect of the elements and things found in nature. God warned His people not to go after the gods of the heathen, but, because of their lusts, they were given over to their own pagan desires. Throughout the bible, from the very beginning, God warned His followers not to go after the customs of the people around them.

Christmas started with the sun worshippers in the time of Nimrod, the man who supervised the building of the Tower of Babel Halff, 3. During the time of Noah, after the flood, men began to migrate from the east. *And it came to pass, as they traveled from the east, that they found a plain in the land of Shinar; and they dwelt there* (Genesis 11:2). It was here that the city of Babylon was built, and this land became known as Babylonia, later known as Mesopotamia. Babel and Babylon are synonymous. Both words mean "confusion." Babel is where God confounded the language of the people as they conspired together and attempted to build the tower that would reach into heaven. Babel was the place where confusion came to hinder the communication of the people and resulted in them being scattered all over the earth. It was the capital of Shinar and was also known as Chaldea.

The bible ascribes the origin of Babylon as belonging to the time of Nimrod. *And Cush begat Nimrod: He began to be a mighty one in the earth* (Genesis 10:8). *And the beginning of his kingdom was Babel...* (Genesis 10:10). Nimrod was the great-grandson of Noah. It was his grandfather, Ham, who looked on his father's nakedness, which resulted in Noah's curse on his son Caanan's line. Caanan's seed did not realize the blessings of God (Note that Noah cursed the seed of Ham through Canaan's line). His son, Canaan believed the curse and provided fertile material for Satan to set up his false religion, whereby he would deceive the whole world. Babylon was the place where all false systems of worship originated. Nimrod was a mighty hunter who gained fame among the people. He organized people into cities and surrounded the cities with great walls for protection. He then formed these cities into kingdoms that he would rule. Despite his advances among the people, Nimrod was an ungodly ruler. It is said that he was responsible for causing all the people to be rebellious toward God. In his desperate zeal to control the people, Nimrod turned their focus away from fearing God, and His judgements, to himself. He became the object of worship and controlled the people by tyranny. Given this option, the people gladly followed Nimrod and complied with the establishment of his government. Although the historical details of Nimrod's reign are not accounted for in scripture, conclusions have been made by historians as well as bible scholars based on a composite of information passed down through oral tradition, legend, and mythology. These sources reinforce the concept that the institution of the pagan system of Babylon was centered around Nimrod, his wife Semiramis and their child, Tammuz.

At the time of Nimrod, the people of the earth still lived in fear of the true and living God, who brought judgement on the earth through the great flood. Because of their descent from the families of Noah, the story of the deluge was fresh in their minds and a present and constant concern for them. The very nature of the flood and its devastation caused them to both seek protection and find assurance that they would not experience such a dreaded incident. These people were so closely associated with the survivors of the flood, they knew the testimony of the sons of Noah and were familiar with the true and living God, but they chose to believe the evil, fictitious religion of Babylon and thus became totally abandoned by the Creator. Semiramis, to maintain her position as ruler after her husband's death, recognized fertile ground in the faint hearts of the fearful people, to institute the false system of sun worship. Her religious premise was to appeal to the sun by paying homage to it in hopes that it would shine or remain present to discourage the clouds that brought the rain. Within this system Semiramis became known as the Queen of Heaven.

Thousands of years before Jesus was born, the heathen in every country observed December 25th as the birthday of a god who was called the sun god. Semiramis, the widow of Nimrod was his mother. She claimed to be the queen of heaven. And she had a son who was supposed to have been born on December 25th, his name was Tammuz. According to all the heathen religions of that time, Tammuz had a miraculous birth; and for centuries, his birthday was celebrated with feasts, revelry and drunken orgies. Halff, 4.

The widowed Semiramis was determined to maintain control of the people by instituting a religion to worship the sun. Her husband Nimrod was supposedly killed by a wild boar, and she became pregnant after his death. Her explanation for the child that she carried was that he was the re-incarnation of Nimrod. Tammuz was the child's name and was presented to the people as the sun god. Tammuz was worshipped by the people under the rulership of Semiramis at Babylon initially, but the "religion" spread the world over. As a mystery religion, many symbols and objects were put in place to be utilized in the worship of Tammuz. The sun god worship extended over the centuries and attracted people of many regions. Even the Israelites were caught up in the deceptive practice which provoked God to anger.

A close look at God's revelation to Ezekiel, demonstrates His disdain over what His people were doing. *He said also unto me, Turn thee yet again, and thou shalt see greater abominations that they do. Then he brought me to the door of the gate of the LORD'S house which was toward the north; and, behold, there sat women weeping for Tammuz. Then said he unto me, Hast thou seen this, O son of man? turn thee yet again, and thou shalt see greater abominations than these. And he brought me into the inner court of the*

LORD'S house, and, behold, at the door of the temple of the LORD, between the porch and the altar, were about five and twenty men, with their backs toward the temple of the LORD, and their faces toward the east; and they worshipped the sun toward the east. Then he said unto me, Hast thou seen this, O son of man? Is it a light thing to the house of Judah that they commit the abominations which they commit here (Ezekiel 8:13-18).

These people were so closely associated with the survivors of the flood, they knew the testimony of the sons of Noah and were familiar with the true and living God, but they chose to believe the evil, fictitious religion of Babylon and thus became totally abandoned by the Creator. Thousands of years later, Paul gave a description that fit the people of Babylon. *Because that, when they knew God, they glorified Him not as God, neither were thankful; but became vain in their own imaginations, and their foolish heart was darkened. Professing themselves to be wise, they became fools and changed the glory of the uncorruptible God into an image made like to corruptible man, and to birds, and to four-footed beasts, and creeping things. Wherefore God also gave them up to uncleanness through the lust of their own hearts, to dishonor their own bodies between themselves. Who changed the truth of God into a lie and worshipped and served the creature more than the Creator, who is blessed forever Amen* (Romans 1:21-25).

The generations of earth dwellers were aware of the Almighty God, but they became foolish. They failed to retain the knowledge of God and did as they pleased. God pronounced judgment, executing His wrath upon ungodliness. *For this cause, God gave them up unto vile affections for even their women did change the natural use into that which is against nature: And likewise, also the men, leaving the natural use of the woman, burned in their lust one toward another; men with men working that which is unseemly, and receiving in themselves that recompence of their error which was meet. ... And even as they did not like to retain God in their knowledge, God gave them over to a reprobate mind, to do those things which are not convenient... Without understanding, covenant breakers, without natural affection, implacable, and unmerciful* (Romans 1:26-31).

Babylon was the place of confusion. It was there Satan invented his anti-Christ religion, comprised of all that is abominable in the sight of God. The people welcomed this new system, that provided room for the expression of their lusts. The seed of evil and wickedness began with mankind's refusal to acknowledge God. The spread of this evil religion of Babylonian idolatry overflowed from its original location in the plains of Shinar, to the ends of the earth and throughout world history. It was in Babylon that the tower of Babel was conceived, and it was also there that God intervened in the plans of the people to build the structure that would extend into the heavens, far above the earth. Very careful attention must be paid to the account of the scripture concerning the mentality of the generations close to the flood.

In the garden of Eden, Satan approached Eve with the proposition that if she would eat of *the tree in the midst of the garden*, she ...shall not surely die. *For God doth know that in the day ye eat thereof, then your eyes shall be opened, and ye shall be as gods, knowing good and evil (Genesis 3:4, 5).* From the very beginning, he came to counter that which God had already spoken. We can be assured that Satan knows what the word of God says. In Babylon, he again found a way to thwart the plan of God by filling the minds of the people with fear and concerns for their safety. After they had migrated to the east, into the plain of the land of Shinar, *...they said one to another, 'Go to, let us make brick, and burn them thoroughly,' And they had brick for stone and slime had they for mortar. And they said, 'Go to let us build a city and a tower, whose top may reach unto heaven' and 'let us make a name lest we be scattered abroad upon the face of the whole earth' (Genesis 11:3,4).* The concern that they, "be scattered... upon the face of the whole earth," is notable. We can be sure that Satan placed this concept in their minds even before it happened. *And the Lord came down to see the city and tower which the children of men built. And the Lord said, "Behold, the people is one, and they have all one language; and this they began to do; and now nothing will be restrained from them, which they have imagined to do. Go to, let us go down, and there confound their language, that they may not understand one another's speech. So, the Lord scattered them abroad from thence upon the face of all the earth: and they left off to build the city. Therefore, is the name of it called Babel; because the Lord did there confound the language of all the earth: And all from thence did the Lord scatter them abroad upon the face of all the earth (Genesis 11:5-9).*

In Babel, the confusion of tongues came from the Lord. The people could no longer communicate their plans to one another. The city and the tower were never finished, and the people were scattered all over the face of the earth. When the people were removed from their original land and language, they carried with them their culture and religious practices. Thus, the evil system devised by Satan was spread all over the world. Therefore, with Babylon as the source of the false religions of the ancient world, we can see the origin of the similarities found in cultures throughout the world concerning objects, and images of idolatrous worship. The celebration of what we know as Christmas has its root of origin here also. *According to all the heathen religions of that time, Tammuz had a miraculous birth; and for centuries his birthday was celebrated with feasts, revelry, and drunken orgies. It was on December 25th that all the pagan religions celebrated the birthday of Tammuz, the sun god.* Halff, 4.

Even where the sun was the favorite object of worship, as in Babylon itself, and elsewhere, at this festival, he was not merely worshipped as the orb of the day, but as a god incarnate. It was an essential principal of the Babylonian system that the sun, or Baal, was the one and only god. When Tammuz was worshipped as a god incarnate, it also implied that he was an incarnation of the sun. It was no mere astronomical festival then, that the pagans celebrated the winter solstice. Hislop, 97.

The winter solstice is the time of the year when the sun is at the farthest point from the equator. The festival celebrated the sun's completion of its yearly course, as well as the beginning of a new cycle. It was understood then that the celebration of the winter solstice was the essence of the festival of the Grand Deliverer, the sun god, Baal, or Tammuz. Throughout the world, this winter festival is celebrated and although there may be slight variations, the theme is still intact. Satan is the force behind the celebration of the sun god, which causes people to disobey and dishonor the God who created the sun.

Far and wide in the realms of paganism was the birthday observed. Tammuz was considered a god, as well as the sun. Tradition claims that his mother, Semiramis was behind the orchestration of the myth of his birth. After her husband, Nimrod died, her child, Tammuz was born. Tammuz was said to be the reincarnated Nimrod and Semiramis is claimed to be still married to him. He was worshipped as the sun god, not only as it shone in the daylight, but its whole course was plotted, and many patterns of behavior surrounded the sun's activity.

Not only is this considered "Child's Day" to commemorate the birth of Tammuz, or the sun god, but we can see how people all over the world are extremely concerned about children during this season. Many go to great lengths to provide the children with gifts and gaiety, having emphasis in modern times on the "baby Jesus" and "gifts" of the wise men. There are many other aspects that characterize the origin of the Babylonian winter festival as being strictly pagan and not Christian.

Is it any wonder that the Christmas season provides expression for many traditional practices to pass from one generation to the other? This can also be traced to the author of the winter festival, Satan himself. Through the institution of the birth of the sun god and its worship, the enemy of God has opened a door of deception that would infiltrate the Christian church and eventually lead many would-be believers into an eternity separated from God. For this cause, God entered a covenant with Abraham. He still needed a people that would worship and serve Him amid a world of ungodly heathen.

GOD'S COVENANT PEOPLE

Now the Lord said unto Abraham, *"get thee out of thy country, and from thy kindred, and from thy father's house, unto a land that I will shew thee: And I will make thee a great nation, and I will bless thee, and make thy name great; and thou shalt be a blessing: And I will bless them that bless thee, and curse them that curse thee; and in thee shall all families of the earth be blessed (Genesis 12:1-3)."* It is significant to note here that Abraham's desire to be obedient to God's call on his life was not easy. He was to depart from his family, including his father and other relatives. As he left his land of origin, Ur of the Chaldees attempting to follow the leading of the Lord, Abraham was accompanied by Terah, his father, Nahor, his brother, and nephew Lot. Abraham's travel plans were delayed at Haran until his father Terah died.

After the death of his father, Abraham proceeded towards the land that God had prepared for him. Taking with him, his wife Sarai and Lot. It was not until Lot and Abraham separated, did the Lord show him the land that He had prepared for him, and confirmed the promise. This covenant that God made with Abraham secured a people to express Himself. It was through Abraham's seed that the lineage of Jesus Christ, the savior was born.

Anyone who believes that (1) God sent His only begotten Son, Jesus into the world to express His life and will; (2) That Jesus laid down His life by shedding His blood and dying on the cross of Calvary as the final sacrifice for the sin of the whole world; (3) That God raised Jesus from the dead, (4) And that He is alive forevermore, are the children of God by faith in Jesus Christ *(Galatians 3:26)*. The plan of God with reference to Jesus (Salvation) and the sacrifice that He made, opens fellowship with our Creator. The covenant of Abraham extends to all who believe in God through the Lord Jesus Christ.

God intended for His people to represent Him. He continually warned them to avoid the ways of the people around them. Those nations were not in covenant with Him. Their values and customs were derived from their pagan religions worshipping other gods, and not the true and living God, the Almighty. During the time of Moses, God established laws for His covenant people which clearly made a distinction between righteousness and unrighteousness. The people of God were to avoid at all costs the ways of the pagans. His strong admonition was that they remain distant and distinct from the people who were around them. They were to walk in His laws, statues and ordinances. They were to glorify Him.

For their obedience and devotion, God blessed them. His blessing upon His people was a testimony to the world that He was the one that should be worshipped and praised. Their well-being was a demonstration of God's love. The nations around them were to be provoked to turn from their idol gods and worship the God of Abraham.

Serving a God that is invisible to the human eye proved difficult for those who were outside of the covenant. Through oral tradition the seed of Abraham knew of His authority, power and ability to respond to their needs. They were taught the traditions of the law from their youth and were blessed when they acknowledged Him and remained within the boundaries of the covenant. The nations that did not stem from Abraham's seed were distinguished by the laws that governed them through tradition as well. Every nation followed the culture of their people. There were many variances of worship, yet the root of their practice was linked to the worship of the sun in some form.

From generation to generation, people passed down their tradition and continued in the religions of their ancestors. The God of Abraham and his seed remained faithful to His people. Often those from other nations would join the family of God by becoming a proselyte. These were people who left their religion and its traditions and joined the covenant people in the worship of God. This was a delight to God, as the proselytes were accepted and partook in the covenant that He had made with Abraham.

What displeased God, was when His people found the traditions and customs of other people more attractive. Many would turn away from the laws of God to serve other gods. This brought on His wrath. The scripture speaks often about how the anger of the Lord was kindled upon His people because they turned from worshipping Him. They dishonored Him by going after other gods made of wood and stone. The nations outside of the covenant were sensual, lust driven, and limited to the life of the flesh. They wanted a deity that they could feel, touch, and experience tangibly. To them the God of Abraham was not real because He could not be seen. They erected altars to their gods and made provisions to honor them. They made sacrifices that defied the nature of man as God intended, and they followed the instructs of their religious narrative that emerged from the imagination of fallen man. Today, we see this same scenario being played out. In modern times many participate in serving ancient deities and other gods although they call themselves believers in God and Jesus Christ. His people are not to follow the ways of the nations. They are to walk in His covenant and glorify Him. His displeasure with such a betrayal has provoked God to anger.

WITH REFERENCE TO CHRISTMAS

Christmas is a celebration of the Winter Festival. Many believe that Christians are supposed to celebrate Christmas because it is the birthday of Jesus Christ. This was taught to generations of people who believe in God. Those are people who have accepted Jesus into their lives with a conscious understanding that He died on the cross to forgive our sin and give us access to the Kingdom of Heaven. This brings us into good standing with our Heavenly Father. Because we believe in His provision for our reconciliation, no longer are we shut out from the joys of serving and fellowshipping with the true and living God. Through God's plan of salvation, humanity has opportunity to join the family of God. We become heirs to all the promises that He made to faithful Abraham.

We know that God remains steadfast. He does not change. Therefore, we must consider ourselves in reference to our relationship with Him. The nations surrounding the covenant people served other gods made of natural resources, like wood and stone with which they crafted idols and served them. They worshipped fire and used water and other materials to fulfill their traditions. It was forbidden for God's people to join them. And His wrath was against them if they did. They were to remain a separate and holy people. If God does not change, it would be consistent that believers today should be mindful of falling into the trap of worshipping and practicing in the manner of those outside of the covenant. Although many want to believe that celebrating Christmas is a good thing, the truth must be told concerning the origin of the holiday and the practices that have been woven into the tapestry of the Christian culture during the Winter Festival.

OBJECTS OF THE CELEBRATION

THE CHRISTMAS TREE

Th he tree plays center stage in the celebration of the Christmas season, yet its use is not a modern invention.

Ancient pre-Christian winter festivals used greenery, lights and fires to symbolize life and warmth during cold and darkness of winter. These usages, like gift-giving, have also persisted. The most splendid symbol of a modern Christmas is the brilliantly decorated evergreen tree with strings of multi-colored lights. The use of evergreens and wreaths as symbols of life was an ancient custom of the Egyptians, Chinese, and Hebrews, among other people. Tree worship was a common feature among the Teutonic and Scandinavian peoples of Northern Europe before their conversion to Christianity. They decorated houses and barns with evergreens at the new year to scare away demons, and they often set up trees for the birds in the winter. For these Northern Europeans, this winter celebration was the happiest time of the year because it signified the shortest day of the year. After December 21ˢᵗ had passed, they knew the days would start to get longer and brighter (Compton's Interactive Encyclopedia, CDROM, Christmas).

Hislop's findings on this idolatrous practice of tree worship are worthy of note. *In Egypt, that tree was a palm tree: In Rome, it was the fir: The palm tree, denoting the pagan messiah, Baal-Tamar, the fir, referring to him as Baal-Berith. The mother of Adonis, the sun god... was mystically said to have been changed into a tree and when in that state, was said to have brought forth her divine son. If the mother was a tree, the son had to be recognized as "the man the Branch." And this entirely accounts for the putting of the Yule Log into the fire on Christmas Eve and the appearance of the Christmas tree on the next morning. As Zero Ashta, "The seed of the woman," which name also signified Ignigena, or "born of the fire", he must enter the fire on "Mother Night" that he may be born out of the next day as "The Branch of God," or "the tree that brings all divine gifts to men". But why it may be asked does he enter the fire under the symbol of a log? To understand this, it must be remembered that the divine child born at the winter solstice, was born as a new incarnation of the "great god" (after that god had been cut into pieces) ... Now, the "great god" cut off in the midst of his power and glory, was symbolized as a huge tree, stripped of all its branches and cut down almost to the ground. The Christmas tree, as has been stated, was generally at Rome a different tree, even a fir tree. But the very same idea implied in the palm tree was implied in the Christmas fir, for that covertly symbolized the newborn god as Baal Berith, "Lord of the Covenant."* Hislop, 98.

"The Christmas tree was introduced into England early in the 19th century and it was popularized by Prince Albert, the German husband of Queen Victoria. The tree was decorated with candles, paper chains and fancy cakes that were hung from the branches on ribbons. German settlers brought the Christmas tree custom to the American colonies in the 17th Century. The use of evergreens for wreaths and other decorations arose in Northern Europe, Italy and Spain. Other nations used flowers instead. Holly, with its prickly leaves and red berries, came into holiday use because it reminded people of the crown of thorns worn by Jesus on the way to His execution – the berries symbolizing droplets of Blood." Compton's

The varied use of the tree in celebrating the Winter Solstice Festival has its origin in pagan Babylonian tradition. God knew that this would happen, and He warned His people not to have anything to do with the practice of the surrounding nations. He forbade His people to take part in them. *Learn not the way of the heathen and be not dismayed at the signs of the heaven; for the heathen are dismayed at them. For the customs of the people are vain: For one cutteth a tree out of the forest, the work of the hands of the workman, with the axe. They deck it with silver and with gold; they fasten it with nails and with hammers, that it move not. They are upright as the palm tree, but speak not: They must needs be borne, because they cannot go. Be not afraid of them; for they cannot do evil, neither also is it in them to do good… the stock is a doctrine of vanities* (Jeremiah 10:2-5, 8). If God did not want the Hebrews to have anything to do with the "doctrine of vanities" should Bible-believing Christians get involved with it?

THE MISTLETOE

The previous references show how the tree plays an important part in the winter festival. Now we will look at another festive custom worthy of mention, the mistletoe. Most modern Christmas party-givers always include the mistletoe in their décor. It is placed over passages and doorways where people will pass as they mix and mingle during the gathering. When two people of the opposite sex randomly get caught under the mistletoe at the same time, they must kiss each other, while others watch. The custom is supposed to bring fun and excitement to the festivities. Many people do not realize that this practice has a deeper meaning. In many pagan traditions, the mistletoe bough was representative of reconciliation. The red berries symbolized the droplets of blood that was to be shed by the redeemer, and the kiss was a sign of pardon and reconciliation.

What a nugget of deception. Man is born in sin because he is a descendant of sinful Adam. As a sinful creature he cannot reach God. He is an alien to the kingdom of heaven. In order to be reconciled to God, man needs to recognize his sinful state, repent of his sins and accept God's plan of salvation. He cannot save himself, because there is no way that he can pay the price for his redemption. Jesus Christ, the anointed savior became the propitiation for sin. He made the final sacrifice, by shedding His blood on the cross thereby paying the price to redeem and reconcile man to God. In His answer to Thomas' inquiry Jesus told the disciple *"I am the way, the truth, and the life: no man cometh unto the Father, but by me* (John 14:6)." When considering the ancient custom of using the mistletoe to represent the role that Jesus played in the redemption process, we can see that the ancients of Babylon had some understanding of the coming savior, and the necessity for His blood to be shed…*And almost all things are by the law purged with blood; and without shedding of blood is no remission (Hebrews 9:22)*. The kiss under the mistletoe offers no reconciliation. The practice of this additive to the Christmas celebration is just another ploy of the enemy to make light of the seriousness of mans need for redemption.

THE WASSAILING BOWL

The Wassailing Bowl gives indication of the role alcoholic beverages played in the celebration of the winter solstice festival. Ancient cultures used a large bowl to contain a mixture of ale and different spices to be shared by the community as they offered praise for the life, health, success and progress of all those present. Originally, this celebration took place during the time of the harvest to honor and give thanks for good crops. Gradually the Wassailing Bowl came to signify the drunken festival that was prevalent during the Christmas holiday season. This is where the "toast" comes from. The Lord did not look favorably on this practice. "…*To pour out drink offerings to other gods, that they may provoke me to anger (Jeremiah 7:18).*" Alcohol is a deadly addition to the winter festival and is the cause of many lives to be lost due to drunk driving, overindulgence and violence.

CANDLES

Candles were lit during the winter holiday season, as they are today. Fire was considered as the earthly representation of the sun to the pagans. Candles were used in rituals to pay homage to the sun god, as well as other satanic practices. Many Christian churches have candle-light vigils on Christmas Eve, and encourage believers to partake in the service. The end of such practices is depicted in scripture, *Babylon the great is fallen… And the light of a candle shall shine no more at all in thee…* (Revelation 18:2-3)

THE FOODS

F ood plays a major role in the winter festival celebration. Over the centuries, like many other objects, edibles have taken on "Christmas" characteristics. Very little attention is given to the origin of the universal use of these delicacies.

THE SWINE

The traditional hogshead, or hogshead cheese, sometimes called "souse meat," is an important item on the menu during the Christmas season. It surprisingly, has its beginning in the ancient Babylonian winter solstice festival. The legends vary from country to country, but the main idea reflects the origination in ancient Babylon with the story of Nimrod. It is said that Nimrod, the mighty hunter was killed by a boar and therefore a boar must be killed, and its head cut off and presented as a sacrifice to him. This custom has been passed down through the ages and is expressed by most cultures of the world. The swine, or pig has become a top priority on the lists of those who shop for Christmas meals. Meat merchants make sure that they have a good supply of pork products for the holidays. The swine is found on holiday tables in form of the Christmas ham. Throughout the winter festival the swine is cooked in various ways to represent the custom of various cultures during this season. Ancient Baal worshippers offered the head of the hog in sacrifice to the sun god. The eyes of the Lord watched as many of His people were given over to adhering to this pagan rite. *They that sanctify themselves and purify themselves in the gardens behind one tree in the midst eating swine's flesh, and the abomination… shall be consumed together, saith the Lord* (Isaiah 66:17). God was not pleased with His covenant people defying His dietary laws and following the practices of the people who were outside of the covenant.

YULE CAKES

Holiday baking is a special activity during the Christmas season. Cookbooks featuring different recipes sell rapidly, as well as magazines featuring the latest "style" in entertaining for the holidays. One would think that there can be no harm in baking delights for family and friends, until its origin is also found in Babylon. "Yule Cakes" were an essential offering in the Babylonian celebration of Tammuz. This practice focused on the mother of the child, who was called the "Queen of Heaven." God detested this practice among the Hebrews and spoke out against it through the prophet Jeremiah. *"See thou not what they do in the cities of Judah and in the streets of Jerusalem? The children gather wood, and the fathers kindle the fire, and the women knead their dough, to make cakes to the queen of heaven… that they may provoke me to anger* (Jeremiah 7:17-18)."

This passage of scripture shows the whole family is actively involved in getting ready for the festival. The word "Yule" is a derivative from the ancient Chaldee word for "child." It gives the inference of the significant role the children play in the holiday season. This is also Babylonian in origin because the original purpose of celebrating the winter solstice was the birth of Tammuz, the sun god and the special attention given to his mother Semiramis, the queen of heaven. God's people knew this, but they did it anyway. *"And when we burned incense to the queen of heaven, and poured out drink offerings unto her, did we make cakes to worship her…* (Jeremiah. 44:19)." We can see that the winter festival was clearly a Babylonian ritual that required specific components. The focus on the children, is significant. They were in full participation as the preparations were made to celebrate. Traditions are passed down from one generation to the next because children grow up and have children of their own. They then repeat the practices that were uniquely prevailing in their home as a child. Memories capture the emotions, and the family customs are found to be significant as the generations move forward. The women were busy cooking the foods, and baked cakes to offer to the Queen of heaven. The men cut down the trees and made logs for the fire. Today we can see the excitement of preparing for the winter festival experienced by the entire family.

THE CHRISTMAS GOOSE

The Christmas goose is also of pagan Babylonian origin. Today, holiday dinner tables display a roasted turkey as its modern counterpart. Many cultures use a duck or a chicken, to worship Tammuz.

GIFT GIVING

Gift giving is an obsession within the Christmas season. People all over the world exchange trinkets as a token of their love and sentiment. Children are especially targeted in this area of the winter celebration. Gift giving seems harmless, as it would be if done at any other time of the year, but, during the winter solstice festival, it too, is a pagan practice. Christians celebrating Christmas have no idea how the custom came into being. They believe that three kings from the east brought gifts to Jesus on the night of His birth, but there is no scriptural basis for such a concept.

Now when Jesus was born in Bethlehem of Judea in the days of Herod the king, there came wise men from the east to Jerusalem saying, "Where is He that is born King of the Jews? For we have seen His star in the east and have come to worship Him…" they departed; and, lo, the star, which they saw in the east, went before them, till it came and stood over where the young child was. When they saw the star, they rejoiced with exceeding great joy, and when they were come into the house, they saw the young child with Mary His mother, and fell, and worshipped Him: And when they had opened their treasures, they presented unto Him gifts; gold, and frankincense, and myrrh (Matthew 2:1-2, 9-11).

When the date of Christmas was set to fall in December, it was done at least in part to compete with ancient pagan festivals that occurred about the same time. *The Romans, for example, celebrated the Saturnalia on December 17th. It was a winter feast of merrymaking and gift exchanging, and two weeks later, on the Roman New Year, January 1, houses were decorated with greenery and lights. Gifts were given to children and the poor. As the Germanic tribes of Europe accepted Christianity and began to celebrate Christmas, they also gave gifts. The exchange of gifts has remained a central feature of the holiday season the world over.* Compton's

Many people believe that the wise men were kings, and that the shepherds joined them in the manger at the birth of Jesus, but there is no evidence in the Bible that states this. It simply describes the wise men as coming from the east. There is no indication as to their country of origin, their status, or how many there were. Tradition has determined the details of the wise men and cast them in supporting roles in the Christmas drama. The fact that they gave gifts to the child, provided a basis for the practice to be incorporated in the winter festival. The wise men presented gifts to the child, Jesus, because they understood that He was the King of the Jews, the Messiah of God. It was common to bring gifts to kings. The gifts of the wise men were not birthday gifts, and they did not give gifts to one another. In the ancient Babylonian celebration of the birth of Tammuz, people gave gifts to one another. Gift giving is one of the oldest customs of the winter festival celebration, it is older than Christmas itself. Christians today hurriedly shop for gifts to please their loved ones and friends not realizing it is a pagan practice.

RELIGIOUS ICONS

ANGELS

Angels are familiar icons of the Christmas celebration. This addition became a part of the winter festival because of the biblical account of the birth of Jesus. It was the messenger Gabriel who told of Jesus' miraculous birth to Mary. Gabriel also met with Zacharias, the father of John the Baptist to tell him of his coming birth. The angel of the Lord who appeared to the shepherds in the field announced the birth of the Christ. *And suddenly, there was with the angel a multitude of the heavenly host praising God, and saying, "Glory to God in the highest and on earth, peace, good will toward men." And it came to pass when the angels were gone away from them into heaven, shepherds said one to another, "Let us now go even unto Bethlehem, and see this thing which is come to pass, which the Lord has made known unto us"* (Luke 2:13-15).

There are no suggestions nor indications as to what the heavenly messengers looked like, or what gender they were, although it is understood that Gabriel was male. The depiction of angels in art is a concept formed in the mind of a human. Poets and artists derive their images of angels based on what they conceive. Some draw or paint angels that have bodies like little babies, scantly clad with big eyes and curly hair. They carry harps and evoke the sentiment that one would give a child. Other depictions show angels as women, with long flowing white gowns, outreaching hands and wind-blown hair. Still some angels are shown to be strong masculine men with bulging muscles, a stern face and an official quality. Almost all the angels depicted in art have wings. It is understood that these illustrations stem from the custom or culture of the artist. But there is no way that they can be accurate or representative of reality.

In his article, *An Iconography of Heavenly Beings*, *Gilbert Highet asks, "How is it then, that whenever we bear the word "angel" we see a being with large wings? How is it that the image in our minds is a grateful shape with flowing robes, floating hair and a kindly gaze, sexless, or almost sexless, or perhaps with the hint of the feminine...this is because Christian art is a blend of Jewish mysticism and Greek imagery. The Jews...thought of God as being free of all bodily form and His messengers as human in appearance- mediums or diplomats, as it were characteristic for their mission. But the Greeks, or at least the Greek artists and poets, could not think of the divine as formless, with no resemblance to humanity. To them, a god wore the shape of a perfect man or woman, endowed with superhuman powers. And the messenger of divinity must surely have the appurtenances of swift and graceful flight. Therefore, Christian artists, working in the Greco-Roman tradition, gave their angels the wings of victory.* The Pageantry of Christmas, Volume II, Time Life Book of Christmas, New York, 1963, p. 56

The angel winged its way to the top of the decorated Christmas tree during the winter pagan festival. The wings of victory have become a Christian characteristic of angels, and many times they were depicted carrying palms of triumph. To the natural or carnal minded believer, this would be a pleasing suggestion of heavenly beings, representing projection and communication in the unseen world, but for those who desire to be obedient to God and live by His word, admonition is found in scripture: *Thou shalt not make unto thee any graven image, or any likeness of any thing that is in heaven above...* (Exodus 20:4). *Ye shall make you no idols nor graven image, neither rear you up a standing image of stone in your land, to bow down unto it: for I am the Lord your God* (Leviticus 26:1).

The graven image refers to carved out material, shaped and formed into the concept of the artists' mind. It is therefore a rendition of the creation of one's imagination and has nothing to do with the truth or reality. Our Father desires that we understand Him by faith... *For we walk by faith and not by sight...* (II Corinthians 5:7). *Now faith is... the evidence of things not seen* (Hebrews 11:1) *But without faith, it is impossible to please Him... (*Hebrews 11:6). Any image that man can form to depict heavenly things has to be inferior and erroneous. It is an insult and an affront to the Creator to form, fashion and present things of heavenly origin from the perspective of man's mind. The sad thing is that many people believe in what they see. The appearance of angels is plenteous during the Christmas holiday season.

STARS

Five-pointed stars are popularly displayed during the Christmas or Winter Solstice festival. The Christian concept of this object is that it represents the star that the wise men followed as they sought the location of the newborn, Jesus. *"Where is He that is born King of the Jews? For we have seen His star in the east and are come to worship Him* (Matthew 2:2). *"...And, lo, the star, which they saw in the east, went before them, till it came and stood over where the young child was. When they saw the star, they rejoiced with exceeding great joy* (Matthew 2:9). Indeed, the star was an important object in the story of the wise men's visit to Jesus, it is how the Lord guided them, but the description of the star is not given.

Pagan cultures from the post flood era were star gazers and astrologers. Throughout history, the practice of prognosticating by way of the stars has been a very dominant force the world over. The Christmas star has its roots in pagan Babylon also. The lust to worship pagan gods was so strong among the children of Israel, that when they were in the wilderness being led by Moses, they frequently turned their hearts to the worship of idols. *Have you offered unto me sacrifices and offerings in the wilderness forty years, O house of Israel? But ye have bourne the tabernacle of your Molech and Chitun in your images, the star of your god which ye made to yourself* (Amos 5:25-26)." God hated the fact that the children of Israel had so deeply imbedded in their hearts the lust to serve other gods. Their images, or artifacts, pictures and statues bore the star of Chitun, one of the gods of idolatrous Egypt.

Stephen, full of faith and the Holy ghost, reiterated the prophet

Amos' utterance in the presence of the chief priest and scribes prior to his stoning. *Then God turned and gave them up to worship the host of heaven... yea, ye took up the tabernacle of Molech, and the star of your god, Remphan, figures which ye made to worship them: And I will carry you away beyond Babylon* (Acts 7:42-43). The "host of heaven" refer to celestial objects that can be seen from the earth. The symbol or idol for the god Chitun or Remphan, was the star. Christmas tree decoration depict the worship of the host of heaven. Globular balls for planets, lights and the star, all represent the homage paid to ancient celestial gods.

THE NATIVITY SCENE

What is known as the nativity scene is popularly displayed at Christmas. The depiction in the art and sculpture of the birth of Christ and the peculiar circumstances in which He was born, is found throughout the world during the winter solstice festival. Many would think that this is harmless because it does not have pagan origin, but, in essence, it does. It goes back to Babylon in its very distinct nature of "mother/child" worship, which is also marked in many pagan cultures around the world.

Satan inspired Semiramis, the wife of Nimrod to rebel against God by setting up an evil religious system that was designed to counter the truth. This system of false religion would mimic the reality of God's plan, thereby tricking people into confusion. The original place where this was done was called Babylon or Babel, the place of confusion. Again, we see Nimrod, the mighty hunter, his wife, Semiramis, and child, Tammuz, born after Nimrod's death. This is an unholy trinity, whose evil seed of paganism has covered the earth.

On the set of the nativity, there are many players. Most of them taken from the Biblical account of Jesus' birth. The backdrop is a dimly lit stable, filled with onlooking animals, haylofts and feeding troths. The minor characters are the shepherds. Joseph is the proud father, standing by and the three wise men appear to present gifts. The infant, the central figure in swaddling cloth is positioned in a hay-filled troth, or in his mother's arms.

Ancient civilizations used the stage or theater to tell stories to large communities of spectators. This medium was not only for the purpose of entertainment, but to teach necessary lessons of life. Human experience is commonly shared, and this form of communication was the way to teach morals, religion and social behavior. The nativity scene is used in that way even today.

Many churches have giant nativity scenes outside of their place of worship during the winter festival. There are also those who present nativity plays, where hundreds of spectators re-live the story of the birth of Jesus Christ. Some church leaders with good intentions proudly project the images of the new mother and child, hoping to make the point of the miracle of the virgin birth. There are very few Christian ministers who understand that they are perpetuating the pagan rite of worship toward the idolatrous Semiramis and Tammuz.

And the children of Israel did evil in the sight of the Lord and served Baalim. And they forsook the Lord God of their fathers, which brought them out of the land of Egypt, and followed other gods, of the gods of the people that were around them, and bowed themselves unto them, and provoked the Lord to anger. And they forsook the Lord and served Baal and Ashtaroth (Judges 2:11-13). The error here is that the depiction of the birth of Christ at the time of the winter festival, is displayed to enforce the lie that Jesus was born during this time.

MODERN ADDITIONS TO THE WINTER FESTIVAL

Throughout history, people have added to the winter solstice festival by bringing in their peculiar effects. Although the cultural expression may be slightly different, the root remains the same. Recent additions have made their way to noticeable positions on the Christmas bill of fare.

SANTA CLAUS

The elderly character who is described with having long, white hair followed by a long white beard, a bulging middle, dressed in a bright red suit trimmed in fur, shiny black boots and a big black belt, is known to be the famous, Santa Claus. His face smiles from billboards, storefront windows, magazine covers, and television screens. His image is ever present throughout the winter holiday season. With great expectation, children plan to visit with him in stores and malls to tell him what they want for Christmas. They write him letters, prepare him cookies and milk and stay up late on December 24th, hoping to catch a glimpse of him placing gifts under the tree. This character does not have his origin in ancient Babylon, but you can see how he may be an expression of the deception presented during the winter festival. He does not claim to represent God, or Jesus in any way. He has no part in the gospel account of the birth of Christ. So where, you may ask, does he fit into the celebration?

Tradition traces the origin of Santa Clause back to the fourth Century Bishop named St. Nicholas. According to the church at Rome, he was a patron saint of children, sailors, pawnbrokers and maidens. He was a man who sincerely loved to do good to others and he did not want any credit, so he did his deeds in secret. This humble bishop who desired to remain anonymous received a make-over. His character took on a transformation in appearance and became the infamous Santa Claus.

Clement C. Moore was a professor at an Episcopal Seminary in New York. He was opposed to "frivolous amusements", yet, to please his children, he devoted a few hours to "frivolous versifying" in 1822. The result was, "A Visit from St. Nicholas." The poem began with these words "T'was the night before Christmas…" and it presented St. Nicholas as a jolly, globular, sky-riding elf. Moore's St. Nicholas gradually won popularity. Later, a writer, by the name of Nast, in 1862, gave Santa his fur-trimmed outfit and the finishing touches on the merry old soul that we know today. His image has not changed too much since then. The Pageantry of Christmas. Edited by The Life Book of Christmas, Vol. II/. New York. 1963. Times Incorporated. Times II, p.84

The argument can be made that Santa Clause has no connection to the ancient Babylon pagan worship, but, if we look closely at the icon of Santa, we may see some things clearer. Santa Clause is a product of man's imagination, yet he holds a very real place in the hearts and minds of young children. Parents tell their children if they are good, Santa will bring them toys on Christmas Eve, if they are bad, they will not get anything. They are made to practice good behavior based on being rewarded. Also, the child is surrounded by deception, when made to believe that they are continually under surveillance. Santa Claus is supposedly watching their every move and recording them. This must be a weight on the conscious of the small child.

They are encouraged to believe in Santa Clause and that he has supernatural powers. He is elusive and flies by night in a reindeer drawn sleigh to bring gifts to those who are good while they are sleeping. The Bible tells us that God alone is our provider. *Every good gift and every perfect gift is from above, and cometh down from the Father of lights, with whom is no variableness neither shadow of turning* (James 1:17). Santa Clause is not omniscient. He is a made-up personality, a cartoon character, a puppet-like figure. He knows nothing, but God knows all things. *O Lord, thou hast searched me and know me. Thou knowest my down sitting and mine uprising, thou understandest my thought afar off. Thou compassest my path and my lying down, and art acquainted with all my ways* (Psalm 139:1-3).

The error in programming the young child's mind with false concepts and misplaced values will have its eternal effect on both parents and children. When it comes time for them to know the truth about Santa, that he is not real, the fantasy balloon bursts, making it nearly impossible for the child to believe the gospel of Jesus Christ. The Lord only knows how many lives are tormented, misguided and lost because trusting children placed confidence in adults who lied to them about Santa Clause. Children are innocent and the Lord loves them. Too often life hardens people as they grow older and experience adversity. Negative attitudes and misconceptions are bred through life's experiences. Children, however, when they are young, are innocent, humble, honest and pure. Jesus loved the children. *Verily I say unto you, except ye be converted, and become as little children, ye shall not enter the kingdom of heaven. Whosoever shall humble himself as this little child, the same is great in the kingdom of Heaven. And whosoever shall receive one such little child in my name, receiveth me. But whosoever shall offend one of these little ones which believe in me, it where better for him that a millstone were hanged about his neck and that he were drowned in the depth of the sea* (Matthew 18:4-6).

Believers must be careful not to send mixed signals to their children. On one hand, you present the birth of Christ as the reason for the Christmas celebration, you go to church and hear the Gospel message, but then, you add Santa Clause and tell your little ones lies. They believe you because they are innocent and trusting. I believe that God is not pleased with such practices. He gives us a responsibility over our children, and we are required to teach them truth. *Train up a child in the way that he should go: and when he is old, he will not depart from it* (Proverbs 22:6).

The perpetuation of idolatry and lies have contributed to the overspreading of false religion and paganism the world over. People train their children to carry the traditions of their families and their culture from one generation to the next. The cycle never ends because no one puts a stop to it by judging whether the practices are right or wrong. This is especially dangerous for Christian families who are commanded to flee from idolatry. We will be held accountable for our children.

SNOWMEN AND OTHER PARAPHANILIA

Snowmen, snowwomen, snowflakes and most recently polar bears are seen as modern icons in the Christmas celebrations. It is because the time of the year is winter, and many regions have snow. Santa is said to live in the North Pole, where there is an abundance of icy snow. The imagination comes into play here too. Like Santa Clause, snow products are a seasonal draw for commercial enterprise, subliminally suggesting that the public get to thinking about Christmas shopping. Little children are targeted in homes, schools and day-care centers, to prepare their thoughts for the Christmas celebration by drawing and painting images of the icons of Christmas. Snowmen and Santa Clause have been a safe area for protecting the world's consciousness of the winter solstice festival. Without these modern additions, the Christmas celebration could possibly fade into oblivion. Because of pending lawsuits, and government prohibitions forbidding the Christian interpretation of the birth of Christ to be expressed in public institutions, especially schools, we can see how the powers of darkness are set on continuing to deceive the world into celebrating the Winter Solstice Festival. If by chance people get the revelation that Jesus is not the real reason for the season, Santa, the snow people, and their entourage will carry it on.

CHRISTMAS CAROLS

The songs of the season do much to set the holiday atmosphere. A carol is supposed to be a lively upbeat song to set the mood of joy and gaiety. There are many songs that are representative of the winter solstice festival, which go from one extreme of the season to the other. The "religious" songs point to the biblical picture of Jesus' birth, the human need for joy and peace, holiday memories of the past and faring of the mother and child. They can be heard in Christian circles, at home and at church across denominational lines. Rarely is the true gospel message found in the Christmas carol. Very few popular songs of the season present the reason that Jesus was born into the world. If this were to happen, those who claim that Christmas is an excellent time for evangelism would have reason to celebrate. People would get saved, delivered and set free from the powers of darkness; however, this is not the case. The songs of the Christmas season are not of heavenly origin; thus, they are governed by the prince of this world who does not want the eyes of the world to be enlightened. *But if our gospel be hid, it is hid to them that are lost: In who the god of this world has blinded the minds of them…* (II Corinthians 4:3).

The mixture of pagan acts of merry-making and gift-given welcomed the "Peace on earth" and "Good will toward men" persuasion that came with the birth of Christ. The gospel message which is the good news of salvation is never heard in the Christmas carol. Traditionally, the message conveyed in Christmas songs point to the child, or the mother and child, as we have seen in the Babylonian custom of celebrating the winter festival.

HOW CAN TWO WALK TOGETHER UNLESS THEY AGREE

There is much to be examined to discover how this pagan festival crept into the Christian lifestyle, but the fact is, you are not required to be a Christian to celebrate Christmas. Christmas is not a Christian holiday but a worldly one. Christmas is a melting pot of pagan practices mixed with mythology, biblical truth, cartoon characters and institutionalized religious traditions. These factors are augmented by the imagination of artist and writers who, in one way or another, illustrate peculiar aspects of the season. Therefore, Christmas, as a cultural event, may vary slightly from place to place, but the essence and the thread of its pagan origin runs through it. Christmas is of the world.

The scriptures instruct the church of the Lord Jesus Christ, His body, to *love not the world, neither the things that are in the world. If any man love the world, the love of the Father is not in him* (1 John 2:15). This scripture should bring every Christian to a sobering realization that Christmas should not be celebrated, nor any of its rites or rituals practiced. All aspects of the pageantry of Christmas are contrary to the truth that the word of God brings to the world. *The very fact that the world, which hates Christ and His blood atonement for sin, makes more fuss about Christmas than any other holiday, which proves to me that Christmas is not of God. If December*

25th is truly the birthday of the blessed Son of God, the world would have nothing to do with it Halff, 6.

People throughout the world celebrate Christmas, who, for the most part, have no knowledge of scripture, or of Jesus Christ, but they love the winter solstice celebration. *To take Christmas from the world would be harder than taking candy from a child. Let us face it, the world is married to the idol of Christmas* Halff, 6. Because Christmas is so deeply rooted in the traditional cultures of the world, it would be impossible to remove its influence. Therefore, God does not command the "world" to change its practices and pagan beliefs but calls His people out of the world and commands them to have nothing to do with the ways of the world. *Love not the world, neither the things that are in the world. If any man love the world, the love of the Father is not in him.* (1John 2:15). This scripture is a directive, a command to God's people to separate themselves and their affections from the things of the world.

In the Old Testament, God called those who would be loyal to Him and honor the covenant that He made with them to separate themselves from those who were not called. He knew the evil that was behind all forms of pagan, idolatrous worship and did not want His people to become polluted by it. From the very beginning, He offered protection from the evil influence. *And the Lord commanded the man, saying, "Of every tree in the garden thou mayest freely eat but the tree of knowledge of good and evil, thou shalt not eat of it: for in the day that thou eatest thereof, thou shalt surely die* (Genesis 2:16-17)." This was God's protection plan from the inherent evil influence of Satan's deception. *"Thou shalt not eat of it."*

And God saw that the wickedness of man was great in the earth, and that every imagination of the thoughts of his heart was only evil continually. And it repented the Lord that He had made man on earth, and it grieved Him at His heart. And the Lord said, "I will destroy man whom I have created from the face of the earth; both man and beast, and the creeping thing, and the fowls of the air; for it repenteth me that I have made them." But Noah found grace in the eyes of the Lord (Genesis 6:5-8). This grace that Noah found provided a means for him to be separated from the evils of the then present world. God commanded him to, *"make thee and ark...* (Genesis 6:14)." Separation from the world invites God's provision.

To Abraham, God said, *"Get thee out of thy country, and away from thy kindred, and from thy father's house, unto a land that I will shew thee* (Genesis 12:1)." Abraham was obedient to God's voice and was blessed with a covenant that proved to be a blessing to the entire world. In order to receive the promise from God, Abraham had to be separated from his country, his relatives and his immediate family. They were a people that did not know or serve God. They worshipped other gods and made idols and trinkets to pay homage to them.

When he left the place of his birth, following the command of the Lord, Abraham took Lot, his nephew and Terah, his father, they were his kinsmen. He was supposed to leave them behind and separate himself from them as well. Therefore, it was not until his father was dead, "*...and after Lot was separated from him...* (Genesis 13:14)," did God show Abraham the land of promise.

Mixing the holy things of God with the pagan practices of the world are an abomination. It is the cry of the Lord that His people separate themselves from the world and not receive her plagues. *"Wherefore come out from among them and be ye separate," saith the Lord, "and touch not the unclean thing; and I will receive you, and will be a Father unto you, and ye shall be my sons and daughters," saith the Lord Almighty* (II Corinthians 6:17–18).

No doubt there are many sincere Christians who think that they are honoring God by celebrating Christmas and having a Christmas tree, when in reality they are dishonoring Him by having to do with a heathen festival that God hates. As you read these lines perhaps you say, "I have my Christmas tree, but I don't worship it and consequently, I see nothing wrong with it." Let me remind you, however, that you don't determine what is right and what is wrong. If the Christmas tree is not an idol to you, why are you so reluctant to give it up? What are you doing down on your knees when you place your gifts under it? Halff, 11–12

The sin of mixture is deadly. Modern Christians see no harm in participating in the celebration of Christmas because their pastors and church leaders do not preach against it. To the contrary, churches find a high time for celebrating during the winter solstice festival. Church buildings the world over are carefully decorated and Christmas trees are on display right next to the pulpit. Messages of love, peace and goodwill are preached, and the people go home with a false sense of security, never suspecting that they are involved in ancient pagan, occult, idol worship.

LEGS OF IRON

T
oo many unsuspecting Christians celebrate Christmas because they think that it is pleasing to God. They follow church protocol, order and programs, not suspecting that something may not be right. They believe the lie that it is Jesus' birthday. Their eyes have been blinded and they have been deceived into thinking that truth is error and error is truth. How did this happen? It started in the Garden of Eden with one small question, *"Has God said?"* (Genesis 3:1) Satan introduced the thought that maybe God's word was questionable. He brought doubt as to the validity of divine instruction and offered an alternate view to mankind. This was the challenge offered to humanity to determine their obedience to God or not. Because they failed to obey God's voice, they fell into sin and made Satan their Lord. *Know ye not, that to whom ye yield yourselves servants to obey, his servants ye are to whom ye obey, whether of sin unto death, or of obedience unto righteousness* (Romans 6:16)? Because of this life-altering event, mankind was plunged into darkness. But God has sustained a people for Himself a people that would show forth His glory. Even though many have refused to serve the true and Living God, there is still hope that they may one day repent and accept His salvation.

The bible is the word of God. In the word, we find basic instructions and rules for life according to our Creator. It is an "owner's manual" given to us to learn the way of life and the mind of God, so that we may have good success. Knowing God's word will help us to order our lives. if we do not study the scripture to find out what it says and what is expected of the believer, we will never know. We will be blind followers of those who are devoid of vision. Blind guides seek to rule over God's people, instead of teaching them how to allow God Himself to be their leader.

Because the physical nature of God is beyond human visual perception, believers must accept and understand Him by faith. *Now faith is the substance of things hoped for and the evidence of things not seen* (Hebrews 11:1). We know that he is real because we understand His person, by faith in Him and His word... *For he that cometh to God must believe that He is, and that He is a rewarder of them that diligently seek Him* (Hebrews 11:6). All true believers understand that faith is the prerequisite of knowing and serving the Lord our God on His terms. *But without faith, it is impossible to please Him...* (Hebrews 11:6).

Faith must be established in God in order to serve Him. The enemy, the devil, desires to deceive believers and trick us into doing things that are detestable and abominable in the sight of God. The devil uses lies and evil schemes for his plan to work. Therefore, he uses clever divisive mechanisms to fool the true worshippers of God into doing things that will displease Him and cause His wrath to fall. The area that Satan has found extremely beneficial in deploying his tactics against God and His people is religion. This is profoundly serious because God never intended for His people to be religious. Throughout history, you see humans attempting to please and appease their god through some sort of ritual or practice, but all our Father ever wanted was a reciprocal relationship with His people.

The enemy cleverly planned a way to deceive humans by setting up organized religion as a means for people to find God, hear from Him and serve Him. This was never our Lord's plan. He can be found in all creation. He is near to everyone who calls. He knows everything about us, even before we were born. We were chosen in Him before the foundation of the world. Bible truth gives us no option for religion. We are His people and acknowledge that He is our God. It is important to allow Him to walk with us and be our God. We need His presence to remain continually with us.

Through the Old Testament prophets, God gives His people counsel against dealing with false gods. He knows the story of Babel and the confusion set in motion there. He knows of the fall of Satan from Heaven because of rebellion. God is omniscient and he is patient, loving and full of mercy. He is kind toward us. He wants us to know that idolatry is evil so that we can stay free from Satan's deceptive yoke. Our Father validates Himself by His word. *"To whom will ye liken me, and make me equal, and compare me, that we may be like? They lavish gold out of the bag, and weigh silver in the balance, and hire a goldsmith; and he makes it a god: They fall down, yea, they worship. They bear him upon the shoulder, they carry him and set him in his place, and he standeth; from his place shall he not remove: Yea, one shall cry unto him, yet he cannot answer, nor save him out of his trouble. Remember this and shew yourselves men: Bring it again to mind, O ye transgressors. Remember the former things of old: For I am God, and there is none else; I am God and there is none like me, declaring the end from the beginning, and from the ancient times the things that are not yet done, saying, "My counsel shall stand, and I will do all my pleasure..."* (Isaiah 46:5-10).

Our Lord declares the end from the beginning. In the book of Daniel, there is a story of a king, Nebuchadnezzar, who ruled over Babylon. One night, as he lay on his bed, he thinks about the greatness of his kingdom and begins to have concern for its future. When he fell asleep, he was given a strange, disturbing dream. Upon awakening, he was troubled by the dream, yet he could not remember it. He sought for a person who could tell him the dream and interpret it. The young Hebrew lad, Daniel, was able to do it because he was a prophet of the Lord. In the dream, the king, Nebuchadnezzar saw a great Image. The image had a head of gold. Its chest and shoulders were of silver. The waist and abdomen were of brass. The legs of the image were of iron, and the feet were iron mixed with clay. The final event in the dream revealed a stone cut out with hands, and hurled at the image, striking it on the feet and breaking it into pieces. Then, the whole image fell, being broken into many pieces, and becoming like the chaff of the summer threshing floors. Finally, the wind came and carried them away and there was no place found for them. The stone that smote the great image became a great mountain and filled the whole earth. The king was so happy to hear the dream repeated by Daniel, because it refreshed his memory of the vision. He then demanded the interpretation and Daniel was able to tell him the meaning of the dream.

"Thou art this head of gold… (Daniel 3:38)." "And after thee shall arise another kingdom, inferior to thee, and another third kingdom of brass shall bear rule over all the earth. And the fourth kingdom shall be strong as iron: for as much as iron that breaketh all these, shall it break in pieces and bruise. And whereas thou sawest the feet and toes, part of potter's clay and part of iron, the kingdom shall be divided; but there shall be in the strength of iron, for as much as thou sawest the iron mixed with miry clay (Daniel 3:39-41)." This was God's way of showing the end from the beginning. All successive government powers followed Babylon as predicted by the dream of Nebuchadnezzar. The Medo-Persian army overtook Babylon, followed by the Greek takeover of the Medes and the Persians. The next great world power was that of Rome. It is represented in the image by the legs of iron. The two legs depict a split, or division in the kingdom. Some historians say that they represent eastern and western divisions of the Roman Empire. Spiritually, they represent the two aspects of Roman influence upon the world, with respect to the worship of the true and living God.

Rome was a pagan society. They incorporated in their policies, tolerance of religion. The Romans also worshipped and celebrated their emperors as deities. Therefore, the Caesars themselves were gods to the people. There was opportunity for all types of sects to establish places of worship in the Roman Empire. The Hebrews were under this rule at the time of Jesus's birth. They were permitted to practice their worship and keep their holy days unto the Lord, the God of their fathers, Abraham, Isaac and Jacob. Most of the Hebrews carefully followed the teachings of the chief priest and scribes and were unwilling to participate in the pagan worship of the Roman deities.

At the age of thirty, Jesus began to minister the gospel of the Kingdom of Heaven. He taught about things that the Hebrew leaders neglected. He pointed the eyes of the people toward God and their future home with Him, in the Kingdom of heaven. Jesus' doctrine challenged the Hebrew religious machine. They did not want the people to be free from the yolk of their laws, therefore, they persecuted Jesus and had Him set up to be executed by the Roman government. After Jesus' death, burial and resurrection, eleven of the original twelve disciples plus one hundred and nine individuals that followed Him went on to receive the fulfillment of the promise of the Father. The baptism of the Holy Ghost, with the evidence of speaking in tongues, which was their seal. This whole experience troubled the Roman Empire, but it did not become a problem until more and more people followed the disciples, now called Apostles. As the numbers grew, persecution got stronger against the Christians. Murderous outbreaks occurred as they attempted to stamp them out. The Romans found sport in feeding Christians to lions and other wild animals in the still standing Coliseum, but the more they were persecuted, the more their numbers grew. Christians were falsely accused for following Jesus and were brutally murdered for violating the laws of the Hebrew religion, and the claim that Jesus was a king. There were many martyrs who died upholding the truth of God through Jesus Christ.

In the middle of the 4th century, Constantine ordered that Rome incorporate the God of the followers of Christ. Thus, revealing the identity of the legs of iron in Nebuchadnezzar's dream. Pagan Rome represented by one leg became Papal Rome, the other leg. This toleration of worshipping Christ did not bring about a mass conversion of Roman citizens. It was merely a substitution of the pagan gods used to tell the gospel story. As this system evolved, the unfolding of the true nature of pagan practices became more and more evident as having their origin in Babylon.

Many modern church leaders are ignorant of the historical mandates that God placed on His followers and allow their congregations, as well as themselves to be deceived into following the dictates of this evil system. Many of the holidays and special festivals that believers in Christ celebrate have no true reference in the gospel narrative, and Christmas is one such holiday. The Roman feast of Sol, which is celebrated in December, became Jesus' birthday. It was originally the birthday of Tammuz, also known as Sol, the sun god.

After Constantine became Emperor of Rome, he forced all the pagans of his empire to be baptized into the Christian church. Thus, baptized pagans far outnumbered the true Christians. Since the church worshipped the Lore Jesus as the son of God, when the 25th day of December rolled around and the pagans wanted to worship Tammuz, their sun god, Constantine knew that he would have to do something. So, he had the church combine the worship of Tammuz with the birthday of Christ and a special mass was declared to keep everyone happy. Thus, pagan worship was brought into the Christian church and they called it "Christ-mass". Every time we say, "Merry Christmas" we are actually mixing the precious and holy name of Christ... This is not right. God says in Ezekiel 20:39, "pollute ye thy holy name no more" Halff, 4-5.

The iron legs of the Roman empire have continued to filter down through world history, even to the end times, as indicated by the feet and toes of Nebuchadnezzar's vision. This mixture will be in effect until time as we know it is over. What shall we do about Christmas? Leave it alone. Do not touch it, have nothing to do with it. Do not teach your children lies and allow them to find you in hypocrisy. Bring your children up to be soldiers in the Lord's army. Teaching them to fight the good fight of faith and lay hold of eternal life. There is no value in our celebrating Christmas. Touching unclean things and worshipping idols brings about a separation in our relationship with our Father. We as believers have come to grips with who we are and what we are here for.

JESUS PRAYED FOR US

Jesus prayed for us in the garden prior to His betrayal. *"And now come I to thee; and these things I speak in the world, that they might have my joy fulfilled in themselves. I have given them thy word; and the world hath hated them, because they are not of the world, even as I am not of the world. I pray not that thou shouldest take them out of the world, but that thou shouldest keep them from evil. They are not of the world, even as I am not of the world. Sanctify them through thy truth, thy word is truth. As thou hast sent me into the world, even so have I also sent them into the world. And for their sakes, I sanctify myself, that they also might be sanctified through the truth. Neither pray I for these alone, but for them also which shall believe on me through their word; that they all may be one… in us* (John 17:13-21)."

The legs of iron represent a world power that will be in effect until Jesus takes full dominion over the earth. Right now, we as Christians live in a very hostile environment, and must understand that we are in enemy territory. Opposition tactics and strategies of the enemy are aimed at true believers in Christ, but our defense is in His love and provision. *Finally, my brethren, be strong in the Lord, and in the power of his might. Put on the whole armor of God, that ye may be able to stand against the wiles of the devil. For we wrestle not against flesh and blood, but against principalities, against powers, against the rulers of the darkness of this world, against spiritual wickedness in high places. Wherefore take unto you the whole armor of God, that ye may be able to withstand in the evil day, and having done all, to stand* (Ephesians 6:10-13).

The body of Christ, the church must stand. Once we recognize that we are in a battle, we have no other choice. Victory or defeat. *"Be sober, be vigilant; because your adversary, the devil, as a roaring lion, walketh about, seeking whom he may devour* (I Peter 5:8)." The Apostle Paul clearly instructs the church to understand the nature of the forces of evil that are arrayed against the believers in Christ. He encourages believers to face reality. *For though we walk in the flesh, we do not war after the flesh:* (II Corinthians 10:3). This sobering statement forces the church to recognize their position in spiritual warfare. Our new creature in Christ Jesus status places us in the direct line of fire from enemy forces. Yet we are equipped to do battle and obtain the victory if we follow the instructions as revealed by the Holy Spirit through scripture. *For the weapons of our warfare are not carnal, but mighty through God to the pulling down of strong holds; (*II Corinthians 10:4). Exactly how these strongholds are to be pulled down is also given. *Casting down imaginations, and every high thing that exalteth itself against the knowledge of God, and bringing into captivity every thought to the obedience of Christ; And having in a readiness to revenge all disobedience, when your obedience is fulfilled* (II Corinthians 10:5-6)

God's people have no room in their lives to participate in worldly pagan practices. We have been given many mandates in scripture as to how to occupy our time here on earth. We are to proclaim the gospel of the kingdom, not the gospel of Christmas. The pagan origin of Christmas is a well-known fact among many Bible-believing Christians throughout history.

In fact, at one time, the celebration of this pagan custom was forbidden by law in England. In 1644, Parliament declared Christmas to be unlawful and, consequently, it was abolished. The English Puritans looked upon the celebration of Christmas as the work of Satan. At one time, in early American history, the observance of Christmas was illegal. A law was adopted in the general court of Massachusetts about 1650, which required those who celebrated Christmas were to be punished. The statute read, "Whosoever shall be found observing any such day as Christmas, or in any other way... shall be subject to a fine of five shillings." The law's preamble explained its purpose was "for preventing disorders... by observing such festivals as were superstitiously kept in other countries to the great dishonor of God and the offenses of others." After the Mayflower pilgrims landed in 1620, the first December 25th was spent in labor and cutting down trees in order to avoid any frivolity on the day sometimes called Christmas. Opposition to the observance of Christmas just passed the second half of the Nineteenth Century. An article in the December 26, 1885 edition of the New York Daily Times stated, "The churches of the Presbyterians, Baptist and Methodist were not opened on December 25th, except where some mission schools had a celebration. They do not accept the day as a holy one, but the Episcopalian, Catholic, and German churches were all open. Inside they were decked with evergreens." The Puritans knew the truth about Christmas and regarded it as a pagan holiday. It would be good if all believers followed their example. Halff 10

Charles Hadden Spurgeon, the famous English preacher of the last century said, "We have no superstition regarded for times and seasons. Certainly we do not believe in the present ecclesiastical arrangement called Christmas… we find no scriptural word whatever for observing any day as the birthday of the Savior; and consequently, its observance is a superstition because it is not of divine authority… probably, the fact is that the holidays were arranged to fit in with the heathen festivals… how absurd to think we could so do it in the spirit of the world, with a Jack Frost clown, a deceptive worldly Santa Clause and a mixed program of sacred truth with fun, deception and fiction. Halff 12-13

The first century church did not celebrate Christmas. The disciples were never instructed to mark the day of Jesus Christ's birth. In fact, as to the day and time, there is no mention in scripture. The focus of Jesus' ministry was to …*seek and save that which was lost* (Luke 19:10). He came as a minister, as a servant to open to humanity a level of life that they had never experienced, under God's reign. Therefore, the focus was not on Jesus the person, but on what He came to do. Our God, who declares the end from the beginning, told Daniel about the legs of iron that would endure until the time of the end. It is not His purpose to change the world, but to call His people out. He desires for His church to be untainted from the world because He knows that the world is evil, and it has an evil prince who lies in wait to deceive. Many Christians will not want to hear the truth about Christmas. They will continue to justify their practices and believe that they are doing God a favor by celebrating the winter solstice festival. We pray for them. For those who want to be holy, clean and acceptable to the Lord, ready to meet the bridegroom when He comes, it would be a blessing to you to pray about your Christmas beliefs and ask the Lord what He would have you do in the matter. Thousands of believers are getting the revelation about the true nature of Christmas and are separating themselves from it. It will make a difference in the courts of Heaven. Deciding to give up celebrating Christmas will be a blessing to anyone who chooses to do so. God will bless your life and your household. You may suffer persecution, but it is for God's glory.

THE BODY IS ONE

When the Lord gave me full understanding about the legs of iron in Nebuchadnezzar's dream, He showed me how the evil system of deception would continue until the end of time. It is His most urgent desire for His people to come up out of Babylon. I needed to have more clarity in understanding the relationship of Babylon, the head of gold, to Rome, the legs of iron. He taught me that if the head of the image was Babylon, then the whole thing was Babylon. I understood this, recognizing that the members of a body are not separate from its head. Therefore, the origin of the evil religion began in Babylon and although Rome remains to the end time, its influences is representative of Babylon.

I thought about Paul's letter to the Corinthians, explaining the Body of Christ. *For as the body is one, and hath many members, and all the members of that one body, being many, are one body; so also is Christ. For by one Spirit, we are baptized into the body, whether we be Jews or Gentiles, whether we be bond or free; and have been made to drink into the Spirit. For the body is not one member, but many* (I Corinthians 12:12-14). The Lord taught me that the same standard applies to the evil systems of the world. Therefore, the head of gold, in Nebuchadnezzar's image represented the source of abominable, pagan practices in all its might and power. The materials that followed, gradually becoming more and more inferior, silver, brass, iron and clay, depicted the decline of power, as well as the weakening of its sphere of influence. The time of the end, represented by the feet of the great image, is when there follows no world power under the influence of Babylon. This is because the light and the glory of the gospel of the Kingdom of Heaven will continue to go forth throughout the world, pushing back the cloak of darkness, and expelling the lies that have perpetuated alienation from God.

I know that this is not a popular teaching, even among the holiest of Christians. It is hard for people to change. Many would rather believe a lie, than the truth and continue to remain in sin. They are those who are on the broad way that leads to destruction. For those who desire to be obedient to the will of the Father, truth and light will guide the way unto the straight and narrow path that leads to life. Because *straight is the gate, and narrow is the way, which leadeth unto life, and few there be that find it* (Matthew 7:14).

When the Lord began to teach me about holiness and sanctification, I understood that I had to be separate from the ways of the world. It did not mean that I had to be different in outward appearance. Many people think that believers cannot wear modern styles of clothing if they are Christian. We must be careful who we listen to. This is another area that the devil uses to keep people away from joining the family of God. It meant that I was not to place any other gods before Him. In our modern culture, there are many things that can be classified as idols and placed before our love for God. I needed clarity. I was taught that the things that pertain to worship was where many Christians fail. Religious practices and ways of worship produced mindsets that are contrary to having a loving relationship with our Father. I was reminded of the testimonies of the Old Testament elders who obtained a good report in the book of Hebrews. These people knew their God and walked with Him. Amid a hostile world, plagued by every kind of opposition, these men and women did not back down from their trust in the Lord. They served Him by faith. Having a comprehensive relationship with God, they refused to accept anything that was contrary to His way. They Knew Him.

Who through faith subdued kingdoms wrought righteousness, obtained promises, stopped the mouths of lions. Quenched the violence of fire, escaped the edge of the sword, out of weakness were made strong, waxed vigilant in fight, turned to flight the armies of the aliens. Women received their dead raised to life again; and others were tortured, not accepting deliverance; that they might obtain a better resurrection: And others had trial of cruel mockings and scourgings, yea, moreover of bonds and imprisonment: they were stoned, they were sawn asunder, they were tempted, were slain with the sword: they wandered about in sheepskins and goatskins; being destitute, afflicted, tormented... they wandered in deserts and in mountains, in dens and caves of the earth. And these all, having obtained a good report through faith... Wherefore, seeing we also are compassed about with so great a cloud of witness, let us lay aside every weight, and the sin which doth so easily beset us, and let us run with patience the race that is set before us, looking unto Jesus the author and finisher of our faith; who for the joy that was set before Him endured the cross, despising the shame, and is set down at the right hand of the throne of God (Hebrews 11:33-12:2).

Again, let us lay aside every weight and the sin that so easily besets us. Following the way of the world will compromise our testimony of God. Celebrating Christmas does not glorify God it is an insult to the testimony of Jesus Christ. In His conversation with the Samaritan woman at the well, Jesus said, *"But the hour cometh, and now is, where the true worshippers shall worship the Father in spirit and in truth; for the Father seeketh such to worship Him. God is a Spirit; and they that worship Him must worship Him in spirit and in truth* (John 4:23-24)."

Our Father does not delight in His people practicing ancient pagan rituals, He is a "right now" God. He is up to date and way ahead of us. He knows the end from the beginning. Our responsibility is to meet the need of our generation. As we pray for guidance, let us heed the teaching of the Holy Spirit and bring glory to Jesus, remembering always that we, as Christians, are ambassadors, representing the kingdom of Heaven. Let us not send mixed signals to a lost and dying world. As we take a stand for righteousness, others will see and know that our God lives and in Him, we have our being.

When I tell people that I do not celebrate Christmas, they look at me as if I have committed a crime. Christians question my loyalty to Christ and try to categorize my "religion." When I show them that the practice of participating in the winter festival is not biblical, nor Christian, they get angry. Many people would rather give up Jesus than Christmas. What shall we say to these things? *Let both grow together until the harvest: And in the time of harvest, I will say to the reapers, 'Gather ye together the first tares, and bind them in bundles to burn them: but gather the wheat into my barn* (Matthew 13:30). I have found that everyone must decide for themselves the direction that they want to go in. We can share our experience by giving our testimony, or teach in a bible study or seminar, but people will have to make up their own minds as to how they want to handle pagan celebrations.

Some say it is cruel to raise children without Christmas. To the contrary, it is a blessing to teach the children how to please God. My younger children never celebrated Christmas. They never missed it. I taught my children about Jesus. How He died on the cross for our sins and how He loves us so very much. It would be a blessing to all Christian parents to raise their children according to truth, instead of lies. There is freedom and liberty in Christ and the joy of the Lord is enough to celebrate any time of the year.

Modern pagan practices are on the rise all over the world. Increased interest in the supernatural has become extremely popular. Many young people are becoming more and more fascinated with the occult, necromancing, astrology, and mysticism. Fortune tellers, tarot card readers, and prognosticators and such are attracting great audiences. Christianity for many is old fashioned and ancient. Many say that Christians are sending mixed messages because they participate in ancient pagan practices, such as Christmas and Easter. The mixture of truth with error waters down the power of the gospel message. How can people take it seriously? At a time that the light of Christ should be emanating from believers, it is obscured by the darkness of this world. Those who have accepted the Lord Jesus Christ into their lives have been given the assignment to *"Go ye into all the world and preach the gospel to every creature. He that believeth and is baptized shall be saved;* (Mark 16:15-16)." The opportunity for salvation is available to everyone. People must be given a choice to believe God's provision for eternal life with Him, in His kingdom. When those who claim to represent Jesus (God's plan of salvation) make no distinction between the kingdom of Heaven and the world, those who are lost get confused. As ambassadors for Christ, God's people must represent Him and His kingdom accurately. Every believer should prayerfully ask the Lord, "Should I or shouldn't I Celebrate Christmas?"

TAKING A STAND FOR RIGHTEOUSNESS

O nce I gave my life to God the experience that I had in the Lord was very real and profound. I desired to know more about God and Jesus. I was not satisfied with fables and fairy tales concerning Heaven. I wanted to know the truth and the Lord was willing to supply it. He filled me with His Spirit. *"Blessed are they that do hunger and thirst after righteousness; for they shall be filled* (Matthew 5:6)." It was He who led me to the truth of God's word. *"Howbeit when He, the Spirit of truth is come, He will guide you into all truth; for He shall not speak of Himself; but whatsoever He shall hear, that shall He speak; and He will shew you things to come* (John 16:13)." I wanted to know God in a real way. I realized that I was blessed by Him and that I was created to proclaim His word to His people.

I am a prophetess. When I realized that my eager desire to know His will was not originating in me, I took no credit. I knew it was the Lord propelling me toward my purpose. I learned how to yield myself to His leading. I spent many nights and days seeking the Lord in prayer and reading the bible. Over the years my commitment to God has increased as I have grown closer to Him in fellowship. This is what He desires for all His children. Many believers miss out on the pleasure of having Jesus as a constant companion because they have placed Him in a religious category. For many He remains in a church or some other place of worship where they visit when they desire. Many seek His intervention when they are hurting or in trouble. Some cry out to Jesus when they are in seemingly hopeless situations. They call upon Him when things go wrong or when they find themselves in financial trouble. Others run to Him when they lose loved ones. When their prayers are answered, or things change, they return to their previous behavior. They put Jesus back in their box and continue to live the lifestyle that they have chosen for themselves.

As a minister of the gospel, I have seen this type of behavior among Christians time and time again. Often people seek me out to get counsel during times of desperation. I have shed many tears for people who refuse to live their lives according to God's will. They shun biblical teaching, avoid wise counsel and do their own thing. When they fall into traps set by the enemy They cry out for help, calling upon Jesus. It is very sad. I am thankful that He is a God of mercy. He knows their hearts and if it is in His will, He turns things around for them. It would be better to always take heed to the ways of God, rather than seek Him out in times of trouble.

As I studied and sought the knowledge of God, the Holy Spirit led me in the direction that I should take. *"But as many receive Him, to them gave He power to become the sons of God, even to them that believe on His name* (John 1:12). *For as many as are led by the Spirit of God, they are the sons of God* (Romans 8:14)." In my studies, I was drawn to the admonition that the Lord gave to His covenant people. I noticed that many were very rebellious toward Him. He told them not to marry the people around about them, those outside of the covenant. As they traveled and settled in the land that they were to possess, there were ungodly inhabitants already there. Those nations were steeped in pagan idolatry and were detestable in the sight of the Lord. That is why the covenant people were not supposed to intermarry with them.

But they refused to be obedient to God's command. They continually strayed from His ordinances and statues and chose to mix and mingle with the people surrounding them. They adopted their customs and added many of their cultural practices to their worship of God. For this cause, God allowed the Hebrews to go into captivity. Assyrian siege of ten tribes of Israel carried away the Israelites to the north. The remaining two tribes stayed at Jerusalem but were conquered shortly thereafter by Nebuchadnezzar, the Babylonian king. Their captivity lasted seventy years.

The "covenant people" were to return to their land Jerusalem, during the reign of Cyrus the Persian king. In this post-exilic era, Ezra, the priest understood what needed to be done to reconstruct the temple there and reinstitute God's laws. He was met with heartbreaking news. *Now when these things were done, the princes came to me, saying, The people of Israel, and the priests, and the Levites, have not separated themselves from the people of the lands, doing according to their abominations, even of the Canaanites, the Hittites, the Perizzites, the Jebusites, the Ammonites, the Moabites, the Egyptians, and the Amorites. For they have taken of their daughters for themselves, and for their sons: so that the holy seed have mingled themselves with the people of those lands: yea, the hand of the princes and rulers hath been chief in this trespass* (Ezra 9:1-2). Here we see how the people easily forgot their identity, and the commands of God. Even the leaders of the people were influenced to stray away from God's will for them.

I found myself engulfed in the book of Revelation. The Lord opened my eyes to many things that will come upon the earth in the last days and gave me a mandate for ministry to teach His people "how to stay free from the yoke of the devil." From that time until now, the Lord continues to train me to minister holiness, sanctification and perfection to the Body of Christ. The training manual is the scripture. I asked Him, "Why me Lord?" "Why are You showing me all these things?" His answer came in a soft, yet powerful voice, "Because you write. I am showing you these things so that you can write them down and publish My words. My people who are called by My name, they will hear you. They will read it and run with it." I was overwhelmed with the responsibility of documenting the things that the Lord desired to tell His people in the last days. Immediately, I began writing. To my surprise, I was brought back to the subject of Christmas, among other things that the people of God are involved in that dishonors and displeases Him. The Holy Spirit led me to study idolatry and ancient pagan worship. Then He revealed to me that throughout history, these things have remained the same.

The Lord taught me that many of His people are still in captivity in Babylon, as prisoners of war. They belong to Him, they have faith, they love Him but, they have not come out of Babylon. I cried, "Lord, what can I do? If people do not desire to come out, why won't you let them stay there?" Then, He expressed to me His tender mercy for those He loves. He said, "They have to come out, Babylon is about to fall. It is the habitation or dwelling place of every unclean, foul and hateful spirit. It is a hostile environment for My people. Many of My people are trapped there. They must come out."

"Come out of her, my people, that ye be not partakers of her sins, and that ye may receive not of her plagues. For her sins have reached unto Heaven, and God hath remembered her iniquities (Revelation 18:4-5)." I asked the Lord why His people were still in Babylon in the first place, and He told me that it was because they were deceived into going there. I asked Him how were they deceived? He said, "Partly by choice and partly by ignorance."

The Lord began to teach me how His people fall into error and apostasy. He told me to study the Old Testament very carefully and follow the progression of the children of Israel. As I did this, He pointed out that the people who were called by His name kept falling into rebellion by what He called going after other gods. I asked Him why they did it and He said, "It is because of the lusts that is in their hearts. Look around you, I have called you and separated you for my service, that you may build up my people and train them in the way of righteousness. I have taught you not to touch those things which are unclean and abominable in my sight. So far you have been willing and obedient to follow my instructions. In the Old Testament, you will find many of my people just like yourself, willing and obedient, but look again in the scripture as well as your present day, there are those who know my ways and know my voice, as well as the things that are detestable to Me, yet, in My name, they continue to fornicate. They continue to play the harlot with the world, the flesh and the devil. Many leaders, know better, yet they lead my people astray. Others have hardened their hearts toward Me. Many would rather believe in lies than the truth. This is how it was in the days of the Old Testament prophets. My people lusted after the gods of the people around about them and neglected to worship me, their creator, their maker. This is an insult to me. I am jealous. *"I the Lord thy God am a jealous God (Exodus 20:5)"*

I cried when I thought about the prisoners of war in Babylon. I asked the Lord, "What is happening to your people while they are in Babylon? What are they doing?" He answered, "My people are in a place where they can never grow up. This is a perversion. They are stunted in development and cannot grow. They will die there if they do not come out. My people are weak and unprepared for the things coming upon the earth. I have set in the church My ministers, apostles, prophets, evangelists, teachers, and pastors; for the perfecting of the saints, for the work of the ministry, so that the church will grow up into a perfect man, into the fullness of their potential in me. But how will they grow up in Babylon? How can they meet the measure of the fullness in a place of confusion? They cannot. My people must come out."

I knew within my spirit the rest of the answer. Not only is Babylon a place of confusion, error, and stunted growth, but it is also a place of death. There is no life in Babylon, no well-spring of water flowing into an eternity with our Father. Many people who choose to compromise with this evil system of belief will not be found in the Lamb's Book of Life. They will never understand the heart of a loving Father, the confidence found in the word of truth, nor sing the songs of praise and victory in Christ. The psalmist understood the condition of those who were trapped in such a compromising spiritual condition. *By the rivers of Babylon, there we sat down, yea, we wept, when we remembered Zion. We hanged our harps upon the willows in the midst thereof. For there they that carried us away captive required of us a song; and they that wasted us required of us mirth, saying, Sing us one of the songs of Zion. How shall we sing the LORD'S song in a strange land (Psalm 137:1-4)?*

In Christ there is liberty, peace and love. There is also room for creative expression, productivity, and the abundance of joy. Contrarily, those trapped in Babylon become slaves, under the rulership of the evil powers of the enemy. The result is darkness, despair and torment.

THE WORD OF TESTIMONY

I n 1989, my husband and I were attending a church not far from our home. The pastors appeared to be lovely people, who, for the most part, appeared to be sincere in their love for God. They conducted a "Spiritual Warfare" seminar and asked us to participate. Materials were passed around the room, paper for taking notes and a booklet to follow the study. They provided a list of all kinds of idol worship and occult practices known to man. The pastor said, as we reviewed the lists, "Now these are the things we have to stay away from. God will hold us accountable if we dabble in the occult, or worship idols. We have to watch out for the New Age movement as well."

As I listened intently to the speaker, the Lord began to speak to me. "Look at the list. Is there anything on it that forbids the celebration of Christmas?" "No," I responded. "What about Easter? Bunnies? Chickens and eggs?" "No," I replied. "How about crosses, obelisks and religious paraphernalia?" "No, I don't see any reference to those things," I replied. "Do you wonder why they are not on the list of things that Christians must avoid? It is because they are things that belong to the devil and they are the very things that will give him entrance into the lives of my people. Through "religion," my people have been conquered." Immediately I thought about the four horsemen in the Book of Revelation chapter 6. *And I saw and behold a white horse: and he that sat on him had a bow; and a crown was given unto him: and he went forth conquering, and to conquer* (Rev.6:2). "These people are not here to teach you how to be free," the Lord continued, "they are tricking you into a dangerous position of compromise." "Should I leave?" I asked. "I don't want any part of apostasy and compromise. I want to be with people who know the truth and who are not afraid to share it."

The Lord continued, "Don't leave. Stay. This is how you will learn what goes on in my church. You will see clearly that their teaching is incomplete because of compromise." I remained and grew more and more upset. I was so angry at the devil for deceiving God's people, then the Lord told me that it was not the devil's fault. "He's only doing his job. He takes orders from Me; I am the King of Kings. It is the fault of church leaders and pastors, such as these who teach My people error instead of truth. My word is truth." I was made to understand that although the leaders presented a well-rounded seminar explaining many things that Christians should be aware of, their error was in their omission. What they did not say was where they went wrong.

I went back to that church during the Christmas holiday season that year. A giant tree stood in the pulpit. I was disappointed. With all the knowledge that they had about the devil and his tactics, why didn't they know the truth about Christmas? The Lord told me to ask them. "Well," said the pastor's wife, in response to my inquiry, "We all have to make choices in life. I may choose to celebrate Christmas and you may not. It is a choice we all must make. Its personal." "There you have it," the Lord said, "My people are in Babylon because of their personal choices." How sad.

CONCLUSION

Throughout the preceding chapters of this book, I have shared how the Lord, Jesus walked me through the discovery of the true meaning of the Christmas celebration. My inquiries started as a small child, facing the challenge of meeting Santa Claus, and extended to my strong desire to know the truth. I find it amazing how willing God was to answer my questions and back up His responses through scripture. It is a freedom and a joy to know that God loves me so much that He took the time to teach me and allow me to discover true fellowship with Him. I am grateful and thankful to know that God's presence is with me always.

As I grew up and became a wife and mother, I retained questions about life in the back of my mind. There seemed to be no answer to be found among my peers. My mother did the best that she could to explain the challenges that I faced in life, and so did my Auntie. I was blessed to have these two women with me as an adult, and their experience and wisdom was always made available to me. Their counsel did not satisfy the depths of my quests for meaning and reasons in life, but I loved them and tried to understand their perspectives. My sister Pat was still somewhat of a mentor for me as well. Being slightly older, she had a more experienced view of life than I did. As a young woman, I relied on Pat to help me get through things that I did not feel comfortable about sharing with the older women. She married a few years before I did, and she guided me through the issues that I faced as a wife and mother. I always looked to her for information about things that I needed to know and if she did not know, she would find out.

We had other siblings who were considerably younger than us and we all enjoyed one another, played games, laughed, and had good times together. As we grew older, we remained a close-knit family. Our children grew together, and we established set times for us to get together for birthdays, Thanksgiving and other secular celebrations. I was always leery about celebrating Christmas and remained detached from the festivities during that time of the year. When I was introduced to Jesus, things began to change in my relationship with my family. They say that I changed when I got saved and did not want to have fun anymore. It was very hard for me to explain what was going on inside of me. I literally fell in love with Jesus and for a time, nothing compared to my relationship with Him. My siblings had not accepted salvation yet, and I found it hard to make them understand what I was experiencing.

I give God praise because He gave me a loving husband who walked with me on my journey of discovery in Christ. We both attended church, studied the bible and got baptized together. It was a joy to have a companion who could share with me the newness of life that I had found. As our children grew, we shared with them the things that we learned. I began to agree with my siblings concerning the fact that I had changed. I was growing up and maturing in Christ. I was a new creature. My husband's family did not accept the changes that he exhibited in his life as well. But we had each other. Every day we saturated ourselves with the word of God. We studied, watched sermons on television, and went to as many church services that we could find. We literally hungered and thirsted after the Lord. We were like the deer that panted for the water, our souls longed after God.

We rarely met with our siblings and other members of the family because they did not seem to approve of the changes that we had made in our lives. We wanted to share our relationship with the Lord with them and let them know that they too could experience the same joy and peace that we had. But that was not an option for them. Many doors were closed in our faces by those who once welcomed us in. As we found that we seemed to be offensive to them, we moved on spiritually and learned to pray for them.

As we walked with Jesus, He allowed us to go through many challenges. When we thought that all was going well, we found ourselves under severe attack from the enemy. My husband and I had to learn how to fight the good fight of faith and stand against the wiles of the devil. Once we got over that challenge, many more followed. At first, we thought that at some point we would declare the victory, and all would be smooth sailing from then on, but soon we realized that was not the case. No matter what we went through, we trusted in God to be there for us and make our way straight. Because we took the time to teach our children the word of God when they were young, they too learned to live a life that pleased Him.

My heart was filled with joy when I discovered that my kids chose to please God as much as my husband and me. One day when they were in their mid-teens, we had recently moved to a new area. We did not have the chance to meet our neighbors, of familiarize ourselves with the community. On the way home, we passed the welcoming center and saw a large sign that invited everyone to a Halloween party that was to be given later that evening. I asked them if they would like to attend, as I pointed out that it was an opportunity to meet and socialize with our neighbors. To my surprise, I was met with great opposition. They said a loud "No," "We can't go in there. Halloween is paganism. We cannot be a part of that party. You know it Ma." I was somewhat taken aback because on the surface my intentions were really to meet my neighbors. I did not let them know, but joy filled my heart and it brought me to tears. I praised God for giving me my children, and for allowing my influence and standards of righteousness to bear fruit in them.

Over the years, the evidence of our relationship with God has determined the path that our children would take. My youngest would often get in trouble at school because she was very outspoken. After getting the news that she disturbed the class, I asked her why. She replied, "Mama, they are trying to make us believe that we evolved from apes. I cannot accept that. I know that God created man, and we did not come from apes. I told the teacher, and I told the class not to believe her." She went on to say that the teacher got very angry and put her out of the class. The same type of incidents happened at school during the preparations for the Christmas celebrations. She was not shy in voicing her views on the pagan culture that produced a distorted view concerning Jesus' birth. I understood that the seeds that I sowed in their hearing and hearts paved the way for my children to live a life that honors the Lord. My children are grown with families of their own now. It was a blessing to me that their spouses are just like them. They too were raised by godly parents who influenced them to know the Lord, and how to walk in His ways.

Most of our siblings eventually gave their lives to Jesus as well. They finally came to a place where they understood us, and a great door of fellowship opened. My beloved sister Pat went to be with the Lord after succumbing to an illness. She too accepted Jesus into her life prior to her departure. She thanked me for imparting my knowledge and understanding to her, she received clarity of God's word and praised Him.

A few years later, I had the pleasure of taking care of my Auntie, who by then was in her early eighties. She always fussed with me about being so "religious" as she called it. Coming from a family of "staunch" Episcopalians she did not understand why my husband and I were so engulfed with the things of God. All her life she attended church on Sunday, prayed before meals and every night before bed that was the extent of her "religious activity." To her we were fanatics because we always studied the bible, went to church, and ministered the word of God. I loved her so much that I overlooked her comments and prayed with and for her. One afternoon, I went into her room and found her praising God. She was crying and repeated thank you Jesus. I joined her with tears rolling down my face, knowing within my spirit that she was being blessed.

My beautiful mother is still with us enjoying life in her late eighties. She is such a blessing to the entire family. She is watching her family continue to grow and now all her children are believers. As I recall, it was my mother and my husband's grandmother that prayed for us way before we came to know Jesus. We are grateful.

CLOSING REMARKS

This book is not intended to intimidate or judge those who celebrate Christmas. It is a tool to inform Christian believers about the true meaning of the holiday. There will be many who will read this book and thank God for the answers that they have been searching for. Others will condemn this work and call it blasphemy and heresy. The truth and the essence of this book, however, are based on the desire of our Father, who is in Heaven, to communicate His will and His love to His people. Nothing should separate us from His love.

This book is not designed to bring schism to the Body of Christ, but unity. The scripture tells us: *Now I beseech you brethren by the name of our Lord Jesus Christ, that ye all speak the same thing, and that there be no division among you; but that ye be perfectly joined together in the same mind and in the same judgement* (I Corinthians 1:10). It is imperative that we judge ourselves, and all that we are affiliated with in life.

The Christmas culture is a contemporary focal point in America. Because of the Christian themes in the winter festival, many non-Christians are protesting the imposition of "religion" into the holiday season. Corporations and businesses are moving fast to remove the Christian reference in their advertisements. Santa, reindeer, and snow people are rapidly replacing Jesus, Mary, shepherds and wise men. Many Christians are outraged, because of this, they believe Christmas is the best time of the year to spread the gospel, by telling the story of Christ's birth. Well- meaning, Bible-believing people are being forced to take a stand and protest the modern movement to take Christ out of Christmas.

Those who are willing to stand up for Jesus Christ must find their place in this scenario of controversy. Only those who study the scriptures, the bible and adhere to its truths will be found without compromise. If Christians are not admonished to celebrate Christmas, biblically, why then should it matter if Christ was removed from Christmas? The reality is that He was never in it.

With all diligence true believers should study the scriptures for themselves and pray for revelation. God is always ready to provide answers to our questions. As a result of my search, I have been blessed to be a blessing to you. WISE MEN STILL SEEK HIM.

WORKS CITED

"Christmas." *Compton's Interactive Encyclopedia*, CDROM, 1993.

Halff, Charles. *The Truth about Christmas*. Christian Jew Foundation. <u>Should Christians Celebrate Christmas? – Charles Halff (eaec.org)</u>

Hislop, Alexander. *The Two Babylons. Neptune. NJ. 1959.* Loizeaux Brothers, Inc.

The Holy Bible. King James Version. Nashville, TN. 1976. Thomas Nelson.

The Pageantry of Christmas. Edited by The Life Book of Christmas, Vol. II/ The Pageantry of Christmas. New York. 1963. Time Incorporated.

ABOUT THE AUTHOR

Dora Adams has been in ministry for over 30 years. Called to the prophetic office, she is an excellent bible teacher, pointing all to know the scripture and the truth of their salvation. She and her husband Charles Adams diligently work to encourage faith and trust in God. She focuses on exalting Jesus Christ who is the Way, the Truth and the Life.

Printed in the United States
by Baker & Taylor Publisher Services